LAW & ORDER
CRIME SCENES

DICK WOLF
PHOTOGRAPHS BY JESSICA BURSTEIN

Sterling Publishing Co., Inc.
New York

For Kerry McCluggage, who shared the dream and wouldn't let it die, Brandon Tartikoff, who made the dream come true, and Barry Diller, who turned a single show into a brand.

–Dick Wolf

For my sisters, Karen, Patricia, and Ellen; my brothers and their wives, Judd and Laurie Lister, John and Christine; my niece, Hilary, and nephews, Devin and Lucas. And for my parents, Justice Beatrice Burstein and Herbert Burstein, for whom, as a child, I often played dead. They would have been proud.

–Jessica Burstein

Law & Order™ is a registered trademark of Universal Network Television, LLC. Law & Order TV Series is copyrighted by Universal TV Distribution Holdings LLC, who have granted their permission to the publication of this book.

Photographs on pages 71, 78, 79, 81, 87, 89, 93, 102–104, 117, 119, 125, 129, 139, 143, 145, 149 courtesy of Universal Studios Licensing LLLP. Photographs by Jessica Burstein.

Photographs on pages 115, 121, 131 courtesy of Universal Studios Licensing LLLP

Interior and cover designed by Pentagram Design, Inc.

First Edition

Library of Congress Cataloging-in-Publication Data Available

10 9 8 7 6 5 4 3 2 1

Published by Sterling Publishing Co., Inc.
387 Park Avenue South, New York, NY 10016
© 2003 by Dick Wolf and Jessica Burstein
Distributed in Canada by Sterling Publishing
C/o Canadian Manda Group, One Atlantic Avenue, Suite 105
Toronto, Ontario, Canada M6K 3E7
Distributed in Great Britain by Chrysalis Books
64 Brewery Road, London N7 9NT, England
Distributed in Australia by Capricorn Link (Australia) Pty. Ltd.
P.O. Box 704, Windsor, NSW 2756, Australia

Printed in China

Sterling ISBN 1-4027-1092-5

CONTENTS

INTRODUCTION

Law & Order is the longest running drama on network television, with more than three hundred episodes and two spin-offs to its name. Over the years, it has received significant attention from newspapers, magazines, and journals. Yet this is the first official book about the show. Why, you may ask, did I choose to focus on crime scenes to translate *Law & Order* from the small screen to the printed page? The reason is simple.

Every *Law & Order* episode opens with a crime scene, which almost always involves a murder. But the scene is never a celebration of violence. Rather, it is a door to explore the cost and consequence of violence and the specific way that we as a society—on the concrete streets of our urban environment—wrestle with evil and try to put wrong, right.

Although America has had a long romance with violence, *Law & Order* is not romantic. It is stark, gritty, and spare. The show does not linger on a victim; the victim's role is to introduce the dramatic conflict.

In late 1993, in the series' third season, I approached photographer Jessica Burstein with the idea of capturing the organizing principle of *Law & Order's* narratives, by documenting its crime scenes. I wanted, through these still images, to represent graphically what I have often described as *Law & Order's* story: the first half is a murder mystery; the second half is a moral mystery.

Jessica began this project before she became *Law & Order's* unit photographer and continued to focus on it for close to a decade. In the remarkable series of photographs that follow, she has fixed on paper the idea that I had in 1993. And more. Jessica's photographs are emblematic of my initial vision for the show, which originated back in the 1980s.

Law & Order was born in 1988 at the nadir of the syndication market for hour dramas. The split-format structure of *Law & Order* was initially predicated on a business, not an artistic, idea. While producers incur a deficit in creating the original episodes, syndication is where the profit is made in television. It was therefore thought to be advantageous to have a product that could be sold either as a half-hour or full hour show. I was fishing for various possibilities to meet this demand and tossed around several ideas, among them, "Day & Night" and "Cops & Robbers." But, ironically, when I hit upon "Law & Order," I felt that I had come up with a series that would be creatively enhanced by the use of the split-format, not one that would benefit from being divided into two shows to be sold separately into the syndication market.

Law & Order bounced around for a while, before finding its home at NBC. In 1988, the show was sold to the Fox network, which soon thereafter changed its mind, believing that it did not fit their programming formula. The concept was then presented to CBS, which ordered a pilot that was produced but never aired, because the network felt that there were no "breakout" stars. The pilot, "Everybody's Favorite Bagman," made its way to NBC in August 1989. There it found supporters for its innovative style—filmed in 16mm with an attendant grainy quality, significant use of hand-held cameras, very short scenes, a frenetic pace, and a gritty, unsentimental approach that revealed little personal information about the show's characters. In addition, *Law & Order* presented the novel idea of featuring prosecutors, rather than defense attorneys. Up to that point, there had never been a television show where the prosecutors were shown to be the heroes.

Although NBC was taken by the pilot, before they would make a commitment, they wanted proof that the show's intensity could be repeated, week to week. I recruited a group of first-rate producers and writers, who initially included Joe Stern, Robert Nathan, Robert Palm, David Black, Ed Zuckerman, and Thomas Francis McElroy. Within four months, NBC had six *Law & Order* scripts in hand and ordered the show, which began shooting in March of 1990. Throughout its history, the show has been graced by the addition of, among others, the extraordinary producing and/or writing talents of Michael Chernuchin, Rene Balcer, Ed Sherin, Jeffrey Hayes, Lewis Gould, and Kati Johnston. All of these people have successfully developed the show's unique creative concepts—including the show's most distinctive attribute, its strict adherence to procedural storytelling.

At the age of ten, I was captivated by the writing of Arthur Conan Doyle. I read all of the Sherlock Holmes books and realized that what really compelled me were not the characters, as popular as they were, but rather the plot and story constructions—elements that were procedural. At the time that *Law & Order* was created, procedural storytelling was almost a lost art on television. When the show first aired, although it was a critical success, the audience was hardly overwhelmed. Indeed, the television viewers were so used to "going home" with characters, they couldn't understand why, for example, *Law & Order*'s detectives disappeared in the second part of the show. Still, I was convinced that eventually the audience would be seduced by the same procedural storytelling formula that had captivated me as a boy. And I was right.

The backbone of a procedural is its writing: the story is king and the royal guards are the writers. And it is no easy task. Everyone who has ever worked on *Law & Order* (as well as its spin-offs) comes to know that nothing is more highly valued than "no fat" writing—writing that tells the story in which each scene flows into the next with the inevitability of falling dominoes. There are no establishing shots, no drive-ups, no walking up to a front door. Unlike most hour-long dramas, which average twenty-six scenes per episode, *Law & Order* averages a staggering forty. Because the substance of each story is dictated by this tightly structured, highly paced formula, for the writers, there is no room to hide. In essence, they have to create a self-contained episode, quickly getting in and getting out, yet clearly communicating the intricacies of the plot.

   Law & Order's stories are believable and immediate. They're based on real crimes, "ripped from the headlines," and are rooted in a real city—New York—whose streets and skyline have become as familiar to viewers as the show's police and prosecutors. Conceptually, it was always my intent that *Law & Order* tackle difficult and provocative subject matter—which has at times led to problems such as sponsor pullouts and ongoing threats to boycott the show by various angered interest groups. I wanted *Law & Order*'s stories to reflect the fact that actions have consequences—although there are not always easy answers nor clear-cut resolutions; that good, sometimes, but not always, triumphs against evil; that justice is not always blind; that in life, there are no guarantees. Moreover, because conflict is at the core of great drama, I wanted the show's characters to represent varying points of views. In essence, I consciously set out to push the confines of dramatic television.

   A character-driven show, one with "arcs" or continuing storylines, is fine as appointment television that is shown once a week. However, if you miss three nights of that show, let alone three weeks, you're lost. With *Law & Order*, you can miss three nights, three weeks, or even three years, but when you tune in, you know that you'll get a satisfying hour of television with a beginning, a middle, and an end. Moreover, there will be a defined resolution and it won't matter if the prosecutor is Michael Moriarty or Sam Waterston. In addition, an added benefit of procedural storytelling is its timelessness. For example, over the years, the cops and prosecutors have always worn jackets and ties. The costume designers have known to keep the wardrobe undatable, using, for instance, lapels that are not too narrow or too wide. The proof really is in the reruns. The episodes produced in 1990 and those produced this year look satisfyingly consistent and have all benefited by casts of extraordinary talent and staying power, of whom the audience does not seem to tire.

The most telling aspect of the power of *Law & Order*'s story-driven drama is the success it has had with its two spin-off shows, *Law & Order: Special Victims Unit* and *Law & Order: Criminal Intent. Law & Order* has become a brand and the branding was not accidental. It was the lesson that I learned from my early career in advertising. The bulk of my time was spent on Procter & Gamble business, which owned, amongst other products, Crest and Scope. P&G was the ultimate marketer and they were fierce about brand protection and brand extension. The idea was simple. If you have millions of dollars invested in a brand, a great deal of that marketing muscle could be transferred to a new product, as long as the new product measured up to the consumer's level of satisfaction with the original.

The realization that *Law & Order* was a brand occurred with a two-hour movie of the week called *Exiled.* In the film, Chris Noth reprises the role of *Law & Order's* Detective Mike Logan. In viewing the finished product, we decided to heighten the connection to *Law & Order* by holding to the show's photographic palette and style. The movie subsequently aired as *Exiled: A Law & Order Movie* and was a critical and ratings success. A pact was found to exist between the audience and the producers—the viewers would watch a movie or a show that was branded "Law & Order" as long as it lived up to their preconceptions as to the quality of what the brand really represented.

Although the spin-off shows differ in content from each other, as well as from *Law & Order* itself, what fuses them together is powerful and distinctive. Each includes what has become part of the audience's collective unconscious: Mike Post's unmistakable theme music, the black locale cards with the accompanying "ching-ching," and Steve Zirnkilton's rumbling baritone introduction, "In the criminal justice system. . . ." And each is marked by *Law & Order's* visual tautness and scarcity.

The hallmark look of *Law & Order* is the work of a string of world-class cinematographers—Ernest Dickerson, Constantine Makris, and John Beymer—who have mastered the art of the neutral camera. The camera sees what the police and prosecutors see—nothing more. Although the camera is a vital adjunct to the entire *Law & Order* creative philosophy, it never calls attention to itself. Its job is to tell the story as simply and as directly as possible.

The photographs in this book capture this aesthetic principle of the show. A careful viewer subliminally recognizes the fact that *Law & Order* is the most desaturated show on network television. In layman's terms, this means that in the final stage of post-production, most of the color is pulled out of the picture, leaving a "cooler" color temperature. Thus, it feels somewhat more like a documentary, subtly blending illusion and reality. It might be described as trompe l'oeil or, to cineastes, as cinema verité.

Of course, humans live and die in color, but, when we think of crime and punishment, we want a justice system that is sharp, unsparing, and unsentimental about evil as well as clear and crisp about righting it—that is, a world of black and white. By freezing the moving color image in black and white, these pictures give us precisely that.

Ultimately, the show must locate itself in the gray area of real existence. To accomplish this, I have relied on a group of gifted writers, actors, producers, and crew members. Presenting these photographs, therefore, has not only given me an occasion to introduce the reader to the process of creating *Law & Order* itself, but also to pay tribute to the extraordinary team behind the series.

In August 1990, I went to Brandon Tartikoff, the head of programming at NBC, and requested that *Law & Order* be broadcast in black and white. Brandon just smiled and said that he'd be happy to put a "super" on the screen saying that if you wanted to see *Law & Order* in black and white, turn your color knob all the way to the left. It has been many years, but, here, finally, is the way *Law & Order* was meant to be seen. In black and white.

CHAPTER: 1

ANATOMY OF A CRIME SCENE

EXAMINING A CRIME SCENE

The *Law & Order* crime scene, known as the "Teaser," begins every episode and plays before the show's opening credits. The Teaser consists of two scenes:

Scene 1: Discovery of the body by "civilians"

Scene 2: The "Aftermath," which brings the arrival of the *Law & Order* detectives and, per the script, the arrival of various players: an assistant medical examiner (ME), uniformed officers ("Unis"), an emergency medical unit (EMU), and by-standers ("looky-loos"). The Aftermath often includes assorted vehicles such as ambulances, police cars, and fire trucks. When the scene is an "exterior," genuine New York City police officers who are part of the NYPD Movie/TV Unit are also present. Although details of a crime scene vary for each episode, *Law & Order* fans know that the Aftermath has one constant: Detective Lennie Briscoe always gets the last word.

To understand how a crime scene is constructed is to understand how *Law & Order* itself is produced. To this end, this chapter will examine the process of creating the crime scene from one specific episode, "Oxymoron."

"OXYMORON": A SYNOPSIS

A young woman is discovered murdered on a street in an upscale neighborhood. At first, Detectives Lennie Briscoe (Jerry Orbach) and Ed Green (Jesse Martin) believe that she may have been a call girl, but soon learn that she was, in fact, a doctor—a cosmetic dermatologist with a high-end clientele. The detectives discover that she had been selling a designer drug called Oxycodone to her social contacts, collaborating with a young Eastern European mobster who supplied her with false names for prescriptions—names that were taken from stolen credit cards. Realizing that she was in too deep, the woman tried to extricate herself from the situation, refusing to continue to participate and, as a result, was murdered.

With enough evidence to prosecute the young mobster for her murder, it appears to be a prima facie case until a wrinkle appears. The mobster, in return for immunity, offers the prosecutors information on a bigger fish—his own father. However, a visit from a U.S. attorney reveals that the federal government has been building its own case against the mobster's father for narcotics trafficking and homicide—a case that the Feds don't want interrupted. In a final twist, the father offers to spill all the beans, including information on obtaining chemicals to build explosives, also in exchange for immunity. The Feds want to accept the offer; however, they've got a problem: the genesis of the case was the murder of the young doctor, which falls under the jurisdiction of the district attorney's office in New York City. The district attorney, Nora Lewin (Dianne Wiest), and the assistant district attorneys, Jack McCoy (Sam Waterston) and Serena Southerlyn (Elisabeth Röhm), are suspicious that the young mobster and his father had,

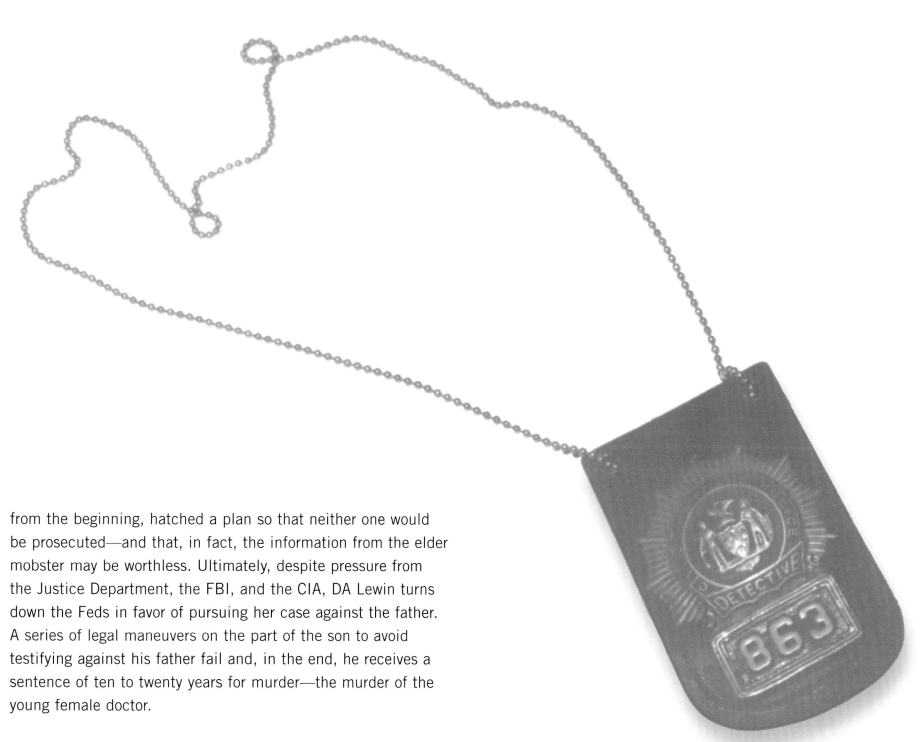

from the beginning, hatched a plan so that neither one would be prosecuted—and that, in fact, the information from the elder mobster may be worthless. Ultimately, despite pressure from the Justice Department, the FBI, and the CIA, DA Lewin turns down the Feds in favor of pursuing her case against the father. A series of legal maneuvers on the part of the son to avoid testifying against his father fail and, in the end, he receives a sentence of ten to twenty years for murder—the murder of the young female doctor.

"Oxymoron" initial airdate: May 15, 2002

LAW & ORDER

"OXYMORON"

TEASER

FADE IN

1   EXT. SIDE STREET - UPPER WEST SIDE - EARLY MORNING   1

Two women, late 30's, in sweats, holding yoga mats, walk to
an early morning class.

                    SARAH
          Tracy's been doing really well since
          John left.

                    JULIE
          I would have gone to pieces. Ten
          years, two kids, he leaves her for a
          private trainer?

                    SARAH
          That's what I'm saying. She hasn't
          gone to pieces. She's a rock.

                    JULIE
          Maybe they just weren't meant to be
          together.

They cross the street.

                    SARAH
              (nods)
          I read that when you meet someone you
          make a subconscious contract... when
          the terms of the contract are met, the
          relationship automatically dissolves.

                    JULIE
          Sounds like a business deal to me.

Julie swings around a parked car, stops suddenly. Sarah
looks, sees what she's staring at: A Woman, late 20's,
wearing a leather miniskirt, high heels, and a cashmere coat,
lies sprawled on the street between two parked cars. Dead.

                    SARAH
          Julie...

Off Sarah--

                                        CUT TO

---

2   EXT. SIDE STREET - UPPER WEST SIDE - DAY   2

Crime scene tape, Unis, activity everywhere. Briscoe and
Green are with ASSISTANT M.E. BORAK who's kneeling over the
victim.

                    BRISCOE
          All dressed up and no where to go.

                    GREEN
              (to M.E.)
          Anyone call SVU?

                    BORAK
          No evidence of a sex crime I can see.

                    BRISCOE
          So what happened?

Borak turns the side of the woman's face.

                    BORAK
          Mucus in the nostrils. Petechial
          hemorrhages.

                    GREEN
          Strangled.

Borak brushes back the victim's hair, exposing a deep, thin,
furrow encircling the neck.

                    BORAK
          Sometime last night.

Briscoe scans the street --

                    BRISCOE
          Pretty risky to do out in the open.

                    BORAK
          I'm thinking she was killed somewhere
          else, dumped here.
              (off cops; points)
          Angle of her body, abrasions on her
          right thigh and shoulder -- she was
          probably tossed from a car.

                                        CONTINUED

Briscoe squats, peers at the body.

                         BRISCOE
              Nice jewelry, expensive coat, makeup.

Green turns to a nearby CSU TECH.

                         GREEN
              Any I.D.?

                         CSU TECH
              Nothing but a house key and a coupla
              bucks in her coat pocket. And this --

The CSU Tech hands Green an evidence bag containing a piece
of paper. Green examines it.

                         GREEN
                    (reads outloud)
              0-5-6-4-7-8-3.

                         CSU TECH
              We were thinking it's some kinda
              combination.

                         GREEN
              How about a lotto number? A dollar and
              a dream...

                         BRISCOE
                    (off body)
              Dream's over.

                                        FADE OUT

                    END OF TEASER

"Sides" for the Teaser from episode 276: "Oxymoron"

THE PRODUCTION PROCESS: AN OVERVIEW

For each *Law & Order* script, there is an eight-day prepping schedule and an eight-day shooting schedule. The scripts are generated by writers in California, sent to New York, and collaboratively revised and tweaked by various parties, including the actors. The series shoots twenty-four episodes per season, from late July through late April, with only one hiatus of a week at Christmas, necessitating a key ingredient: speed. To accommodate this need, a part of the production unit works in two teams. While one team is prepping, or preparing, a script, the other team is shooting. In most departments, however, there are overlaps, which means that, unlike other one-hour weekly television dramas, people work on a continuous prepping and shooting schedule. This overlap is possible because of *Law & Order*'s gifted and highly dedicated staff, most of whom have worked together for years. The following is the production process for the eight days of prep. Although tailored to the crime scene, this schedule applies to every aspect of creating a complete *Law & Order* episode. It should be noted that each episode's eight-day shoot generally sees four days at the company stages and four days at various New York City locations.

DAY 1: Initial script meeting. The production team focuses on the discussion of locations. They review the Teaser/Aftermath and request changes to the writer.

DAYS 2–6: Location scouting. Since locations often dictate scenarios, the selected locations are incorporated into the writing.

DAYS 3, 5, and 7: Casting for the entire episode. Actors for the Teaser/Aftermath, including the dead body, are chosen during the last session.

DAY 3, 4, or 5: The *Law & Order* cast "read-throughs." The stars discuss any script concerns, including what the "cops" have to say about the Teaser/Aftermath.

DAY 7: The location "tech scout." All the department heads visit the location sites and discuss the elements of the Teaser/Aftermath with the entire production team.

DAY 8: Final prep for the entire show. The morgue photographs are taken on this day, because they play as evidence shots early in the filming of the episode.

NEXT WORKING DAY: The episode begins its eight days of shooting and a new script begins prepping.

THE SCRIPT

Barry Schindel, an executive producer, was with Law & Order *for three seasons, and was the head writer, or "show runner," during the creation of "Oxymoron." There are ten writers on staff. Schindel, in California, created the stories, assigned the scripts to the writers, and oversaw the entire process. (He has subsequently been replaced by Michael Chernuchin, who returned to* Law & Order *in season thirteen, after a six-year absence.)*

Barry Schindel:

For every *Law & Order* script, there's a lot to tell in a brief period of time. The story has to be interesting, has to work for the actors, and has to be accurate and self-contained. In addition, we have to meet the criteria of the network censors, Standards and Practices, and we have to pay attention to a host of seemingly small details. For a variety of reasons, we generally make four to five script revisions per episode and we have to make them quickly. Writing scripts for the series is not a job without pressure. Still, I'm proud to be part of this very successful enterprise.

The crime scene is important, not simply because it sets the stage for the episode, but because it establishes the forensic details for the first and second acts. Although the "Order" side of the show carries a whole set of its own requirements, the "Law" side generates the most controversy with the audience. The fact is that the show is written to be controversial. And as Dick Wolf says, "*Law & Order* is an equal opportunity offender."

The script for "Oxymoron" was written by a freelancer, Michael Harbert, with whom I closely worked. There's always collaboration on the scripts, including input from the actors. Per *Law & Order's* style, the idea for the "Oxymoron" story was "ripped from the headlines" of two individual legal cases. We combined them and then added the twists and turns for which the show is known.

Crafting the "Oxymoron" crime scene was interesting because, in fact, it was truly arbitrary. Although, as with all *Law & Order* crime scenes, it served as the point of departure for the episode, the story soon veered sharply into other issues. Thus, we could be a little more inventive. We essentially created a "victim" whom we felt would be interesting, provocative, and sympathetic. We made her young, we made her attractive, and we made her misguided. Originally, our victim was found dead in the street wearing a red teddy. The idea was to keep her persona as ambiguous as possible, so that when the "cops" begin investigating, they believe that she could be a prostitute. And thus, it would be particularly surprising for them to learn that she was a doctor. In the course of script revisions, the teddy was changed to less provocative clothing. But she was just as dead. And the heart of the story remained the same: how far will people go to make deals?

A NOTE ABOUT STANDARDS AND PRACTICES

Standards and Practices is the area of network television that controls censorship. Although the Federal Communications Commission (FCC) sets the guidelines for what can or cannot be shown on commercial television, the television networks have a measure of interpretative leeway. Each of the networks independently makes its decisions and may choose to be more relaxed about some things and more stringent about others. Worries about advertising fallout play a key part in this process. NBC, which airs the initial *Law & Order* episodes, makes decisions on a case-by-case basis. Clearly, through the years, many restrictions have been lifted, but there are still elements that are deemed inappropriate.

The most obvious restriction involves profane language and is what is termed in commercial television as the "Seven Word Rule." There are seven words (which will be left to the reader's imagination) that, to date, can never be used on air. The impact of this rule is primarily felt during *Law & Order*'s crime scenes. Throughout the years, whenever someone stumbles upon the dead body, the strongest verbal reaction invariably is "Oh, my God!" The show's cast and crew eagerly await the day when a far truer response may be allowed to appear in a script.

Law & Order prides itself on its paucity of violence. For example, in the show's thirteen-year history, gunfire has been shown only several times and only when it was absolutely critical to the story. Thus, it's a moot point for the network. But, NBC does have a policy concerning "blood" used at the crime scenes, which is essentially to limit the amount. The show makes every effort to meet this concern. There was, however, one episode that was temporarily shelved because NBC felt that the crime scene was too gory. (Refer to "Postmortem," at the end of the book, to find out which episode.)

Michael Struk:

The paramount issue for me, when I receive a script, is to look at the police procedures and protocol. I'm very detail-oriented and I try to keep everything as authentic as possible. I begin, as does every script, with the crime scene, checking to see that police procedural matters are correct. Depending upon the technical weight of a crime scene, I look at the details of the ballistics, hair, blood, fibers, and the maintenance of the chain of custody. The same day that I receive a script, I send notes back on the scenes that need adjustments. Generally, the veteran writers make few mistakes with police procedures, but there are sometimes problems with the forensics information. On the whole, however, *Law & Order* plays it close to the vest. I often hear from law enforcement officials around the country complimenting the authenticity of the police work.

The crime scene for "Oxymoron" required only a minor change. The notation I sent to production read as follows:
"Page # 3 . . . re: Green queries the uniform about the victim's property. The uniform hands over the evidence bag, etc. . . . Remarks: A little fuzzy, but I feel like the uniform did the search. Am I wrong? We don't want to think the 'uni' searched the victim with all this talent standing around. Gotta keep the doughnut powder off the victim."

POLICE TECHNICAL CONSULTANT

Michael Struk has been Law & Order's *police technical consultant for thirteen seasons. A veteran New York City police detective, he spent twenty years with the department before becoming a private investigator. Struk's job is to review the scripts for the authenticity of police matters. In the thirteen years that* Law & Order *has been on the air, he has reviewed every single script.*

THE EXECUTIVE PRODUCER

Jeffrey Hayes has been with Law & Order *for thirteen seasons, becoming its executive producer midway through season eleven. Apart from Dick Wolf, Hayes is the show's "boss of all bosses."*

Jeffrey Hayes:

As executive producer, I oversee every aspect of *Law & Order*'s production. In essence, I have final responsibility for delivering the film and for everything that's in it. The process begins with notations about the draft of a script for any creative or technical changes needed. Although I do not pick the stories, I make all the decisions about how we are to "fill out" the script. Once these changes are established, the script is published. I then hire the director and work closely with the episode's producer during the eight-day prepping period that follows. Since we prep one episode while another is shooting, I have a continuous flow of work. I am enormously advantaged in my job by a spectacularly loyal and dedicated cast and crew, many of whom have worked together for years. Producing *Law & Order* is a highly collaborative process and, in general, nowhere else in the show is this more evident than in creating the crime scenes.

The *Law & Order* crime scenes often demand a very sophisticated technical choreography and always require a delicate balance of impact and subtlety. Although the degree of technical elements to be juggled varies per episode, each crime scene has its own challenges. Whether we need elaborate physical staging or very little, our goal remains the same. In a show that is all about

consequences, the crime scene is the most immediate consequence and must be believable for the episode to work. In establishing the crime, what the camera records is a quick view of a "victim" and the environment, virtually a few seconds, for which we have spent many hours of preparation.

From my perspective, the "Oxymoron" crime scene was not difficult. As a daytime scene, it did not require a lighting and construction setup, which are generally the most time consuming elements of the crime scenes. Coupled with the fact that it was to be the first scene we shot that day, we did not build the day's entire shoot, as we often do, around the crime scene location. During prep, we did have some controversy over a change in the victim's clothing, and there were concerns regarding the placement of the body at the crime scene—all of which were quickly resolved. I wasn't at the shoot, because it wasn't necessary. *Law & Order*'s gifted crew allows me the luxury of a management style that is to simply let people do their jobs.

THE PRODUCER

Kati Johnston is one of the two alternating producers on Law & Order *and produced the "Oxymoron" episode. She has been with* Law & Order *for eleven seasons, the last five as a producer. Johnston's job is to shepherd an episode from beginning to end, which means hands-on involvement in every aspect of the production process.*

Kati Johnston:

In essence, my job as a producer is to be the problem solver and final arbiter in the process for each of my episodes. During an episode's prep period, I attend every meeting: script, locations, casting for the supporting actor roles, and the cast read-throughs. I have continuous discussions with our executive producer, Jeff Hayes, and the director. I visit potential sites with the location scouts and have technical consultations with the crew. During the eight days of shooting, I'm on set for every scene, where I field a

seemingly endless number of questions, check details, and sign off on expenses.

The crime scenes on *Law & Order,* more than any other aspect of the show, involve the most concentration and the greatest degree of collaboration. And since these particular scenes vary greatly from episode to episode, the crew has to adjust to a lot of new and unforeseen situations. As well, I find that because of the subject matter, there's a higher level of intensity that accrues to the crime scenes.

From a technical standpoint, the "Oxymoron" crime scene was fairly straightforward, although a script change in the Teaser meant a little more work for some departments. On the whole, daytime exterior crime scenes, like this one, are less complicated than those that are shot at night or as interiors, which may require extensive lighting design. Still, because of the timing of the scene—which took place at the break of day—daylight was, in fact, an issue. We had to have the scene completed before problems would arise with the impending sunlight. And we had anticipated an entire day's shooting schedule based on completing the crime scene within an allotted period of time. The time factor was risky, but we were, indeed, able to get the job done, do it well, and stay on schedule.

THE DIRECTOR

Constantine Makris, A.S.C. (American Society of Cinematographers), known familiarly as "Gus," directed "Oxymoron" and has worked for Law & Order *for thirteen seasons, first as the director of photography (for which he won three Emmy Awards) and, since 1994, as a director. On any film set, the director is the commander in chief.*

Gus Makris:

In the simplest terms, I define directing as trying to find a picture and a mood to interpret the written word. Good directing should enhance, not interfere with the story. During the eight days of prep, I read and re-read the script, developing in my mind images that will work. It's a great advantage that I've been with *Law & Order* from the beginning and, having been the show's cinematographer, have technical expertise with the camera and lighting. However, the transition to directing meant that I needed to find a common language with the actors. *Law & Order's* acting and visual style is lean, its dialogue terse, and there's an economy in the way the show is written: short scenes, no establishing shots. The show's style has become a benchmark in television and, in good part, is responsible for *Law & Order's* success. It looks simple, but as an old saying in this business goes: "It takes a lot of lighting, to do no lighting."

Prepping for the "Oxymoron" crime scene first involved selecting the location, which was done in collaboration with the location manager and production designer. From within the day's selected shooting area (the "hub"), I decided on West 68th Street, off Central Park West. I did a run-through for blocking (or positioning of characters) and timing with my first assistant director, Stuart Feldman. The dead body in the scene is found in the morning, between two vehicles. To help obscure the body in order to create a more realistic "discovery," I requested that one SUV be strategically placed. I also blocked the scene to have the camera shoot diagonally, so that the body would be less visible from across the street.

Throughout the prep, there were location visits and ongoing talks with the actors and the department heads. Seven days into prep, I cast the actress for the part of the dead body. Since the body was obviously not going to speak, I cast her for type. An audition for the dead body has never involved my asking an actor to play dead. I do, however, explain the physical circumstances, so that an actor can decide if he or she is willing to lie down in often unpleasant places. The crime scene shoot began early in the morning and took about two hours to complete. Our actress was a real trouper and, with the exception of a brief break, was on the ground for the entire time. As always, both the discovery of the body and the aftermath were each done in one shot, without any cuts. The camera was hand-held throughout, with suggestions from its operator, David Tuttman, on how best to "stretch the frame"—meaning, what he saw as the best movements to contain everything we needed. Because the entire cast and crew made their usual generous contributions, our shoot was a success.

THE LOCATION MANAGER

Moe Bardach has been Law & Order's *location manager for ten seasons. The job of the location manager is equivalent to being a casting agent for New York City itself. Bardach's department includes two alternating assistant location managers, Bridget Clark and Matt Lamb, and twelve additional employees, including the parking coordinator, Leon Adair, location scouts, assistants, and interns.*

Moe Bardach:

Since New York City is so critical to the look of *Law & Order,* it is always given priority in the show's scheduling. In plain terms, every episode's shooting schedule is defined by its locations. The key to "building the days," as the process is known, is not only to find the perfect sites for what is scripted, but to find them in the most efficient and economical fashion. Thus, our goal is to shoot all of a day's scenes within a "hub" of a few city blocks, thereby eliminating the time and expense of having to move the equipment trucks. Apart from the producer and director, we work closely with the production designer, who is central to making the final decisions, since he is responsible for the overall look of the show. Once the locations are chosen, we obtain approval from the venues, have everything cleared with the Mayor's Office of Film, Theatre & Broadcasting, work out the episode's logistics, and create a location breakdown.

Although the city locations are free, there are areas known as "Hot Zones," where, for a variety of reasons, no filming is permitted. These no-filming zones were, understandably, expanded after 9/11. Indeed, after the attacks, it was six months before *Law & Order* was allowed to resume shooting in downtown New York. Moreover, there was palpable discomfort about allowing strangers into buildings and we had a difficult period of securing locations. The "Oxymoron" crime scene took place seven months after 9/11 and, at that point, we encountered fewer problems and found willing renters in the Lincoln Center area (the West 60s). The day's hub was inclusive of five blocks, from which the director selected West 68th Street for the crime scene shoot. It was a good choice because it's an attractive street in an upscale neighborhood—a contrast that gave the scene additional impact.

The *Law & Order* crew is expert at creating illusions at locations. My favorite location illusion was for the crime scene in the episode "Charm City" (Part One), where we created a fake subway station entrance, bricks and all. The delight expressed by so many passersby who thought they had a new subway stop was just extraordinary.

THE PRODUCTION DESIGNER

Robert Thayer was Law & Order's production designer for seven seasons, after serving for two seasons as the show's art director. The production designer, who is the head of the art department, is responsible for the look of everything except the actors. His domain includes the selection of locations and set and prop design. The job requires that he be privy to every aspect of the production process: script, location, technical meetings, and scouts. Ultimately, the production designer focuses on the big picture, painting the broad strokes, which his team then fills in. (Robert Thayer left the show prior to its thirteenth season and was replaced by Gary Weist.)

Robert Thayer:

Although my goal is to visually translate what has been written, in large part, it falls to me to be responsible for what Dick Wolf calls "the seventh character": New York City itself. When I read the script, the very first thing I have to decide about any scene is: "Would it happen here?" . . . "Does this or that look right—is it new, old, squalid, posh, etc.?" This means that selecting locations is the top priority. I count on the show's location manager, Moe Bardach, to offer up a variety of location possibilities and have these eyed by the director. As the locations become set, I then determine what elements will give the best overall impression on screen and issue the ground plans for work to be done. I work very closely with the director during the prepping period, but by the time that script begins to shoot, I'm back to prepping with the next director for the episode that follows.

Law & Order's stages have a number of what are termed "permanent sets," such as the interior of the police precinct, Riker's Island, the interrogation room, the morgue, a hospital interior emergency room entrance, the district attorney's offices and conference room, and the courtroom with its attached rotunda. On occasion we may create a temporary set at the stages for a particular scene. This has occurred only a couple of times for the crime scenes, because they, most of all, are best expressed at locations. The work involved with the crime scenes, of course, varies per episode. Often, for interior scenes shot on location, we've had to create rather intricate sets. For exterior crime scenes, however, we let New York City play its part. We may change signs and the like and we certainly light at night, but we always let the texture of the city shine.

Law & Order daylight crime scenes, like that of "Oxymoron," are never artificially lit. And from a technical vantage point, this crime scene required very little in the way of design. Yet, I was concerned about what I felt was a script problem that required a serious suspension of disbelief. In "Oxymoron," the victim, who was killed at night, is found dead in the morning—hours later—on a New York City street. Anyone who knows this city appreciates the fact that it would be highly unlikely for a dead body to go unnoticed for this length of time. Ultimately, I realized that although the scenario might be highly unlikely, it was, in fact, possible. Through creative camera angles and strategic placement of the body, the scene was made to work.

ABOUT THE ART DEPARTMENT

Law & Order's *art department is the largest unit in the show, employing seventeen full-time crew members and two part-time assistants. Headed by the production designer, the department includes the art director, the art department coordinator, the set decorator, the leadman (the key set dresser), eight additional set dressers, one stand-by set dresser, the head scenic artist, the set scenic, two additional scenics, a set dresser "float," a full-time carpenter and two construction grips. All of these people work together to build sets "from scratch," as well as to alter pre-existing locations. In essence, this department is responsible for creating* Law & Order's *most tangible illusions.*

Art Director C.J. Simpson:

I've been *Law & Order's* art director for seven seasons. My job is to follow the orders of the production designer. While he creates the overall visual impression, I fill in the details. I draft and oversee the scenic construction, supervise the installations, work with the prop department to create specific graphic designs, oversee the still photography, and interact with all of *Law & Order's* departments.

The most interesting part of my work is the police side of the show, which involves more location work and a lot of varying visual input. In particular, I have a real affinity for the crime scenes since they are ever changing and, thus, ever challenging. The "Oxymoron" crime scene required a fair amount of research for the make-up artists, although less work was created for the scenic artists, which was unusual. I did, however, finesse the use of the scripted still photography of the dead body. Since the crime scene

shoot ended up scheduled seven days into the episode—later than originally anticipated—I added a morgue still shot for the purpose of victim identification. We have much more leeway in shooting stills in the morgue, since these can be done during an episode's prep period, as soon as the dead body is cast. Most often, morgue photographs are taken for use on the show as evidence shots, detailing the victim's wound. In my job, however, there are always bits and pieces to fit and refit. To say the least, it keeps things interesting.

Head Scenic Artist Linda Skipper:

I began working on *Law & Order* at the beginning—the pilot. For each episode, the job of the scenic department is to make all the visual "stuff" that comes from the imagination of the production designer. The project first goes to the carpenters to be built and then comes to us. We do all the painting and give it character—whether it needs to be made beautiful in marble or in finely grained wood, or needs to look neglected, dirty, or peeling. We primarily prepare crime scenes when they involve a lot of blood spilled on the ground, the floor, or furniture, or when someone is shot and the blood splatters on the walls. The only blood that is not a part of our domain is that used specifically on the body. That's the job of the make-up artists. It's a very rare occurrence when we do not have blood to place at a *Law & Order* crime scene. And thus from my perspective, the most unusual aspect of the "Oxymoron" crime scene was that we did absolutely nothing.

Leadman Tom Conway:

I've worked on *Law & Order* for eleven seasons, the last seven, as the leadman, or key set dresser. As set dressers, I quip that we are the "cavalry of the film crew," always coming in ahead, per the scene's requirements. The set dressers are directly responsible for furnishing and decorating all sets on location as well as at the stages. Often, we need to alter offices and residences to reflect the scripted characters. For example, we may have a plain New York City municipal office to work with to create a police squad room. By adding "police dressing," i.e. bulletin boards with "Wanted" posters, NYPD paraphernalia, etc., coupled with bustling background extras, we have transformed the space into a location we wouldn't have had access to shoot in. We also have to be attentive to a variety of dressing details such as window treatments to enhance or control lighting for photographic purposes. It can be disconcerting to continually create murder scenes. But, I think that *Law & Order* is careful in the handling and purposeful about the subject matter. For our department, the "Oxymoron" crime scene was an "as is," an exterior sidewalk, which required no set dressing.

THE ASSISTANT DIRECTOR

Stuart Feldman is one of Law & Order's *alternating first assistant directors (ADs). He has worked for the show for eight seasons, the last three as a first AD, the key hands-on person in coordinating the scheduling and logistics for the shoot. Feldman is supported by a production team that consists of Second AD Luis Nieves, a second second AD, four staff production assistants (PAs), several additional PAs for location days, and the DGA (Director's Guild of America) trainee.*

Stuart Feldman:

During the course of the eight-day prep, I devise a constantly evolving "strip schedule," or breakdown, for the forty to forty-five scenes in a *Law & Order* episode. This breakdown reflects the length of each scene, the actors who are involved, and which scenes will be filmed on location or at our stages. With the input of all the show's departments, I continuously adjust to new information, revising the breakdown several times a day. I start by building a plan based on locations, which, because of the pace of the shoot—five to six scenes per day—dictate the schedule. A location may be available only on a given day or at a given time and so, once booked, it's the last element we want to change. Since each crime scene has its own unique set of location needs, it is usually given priority in the scheduling process.

The evening before the new episode shoots, my department prepares the first of eight daily "call sheets," which detail the time and location of the filming and the specifics, department by department, for everything that's needed for each scene. We also prepare "sides," a daily miniaturized version of the script featuring the scenes that will be filmed on that day. At the shoot, my main goal is to help the director "make the day"—to complete, to his or her satisfaction, every scene on schedule. Crime scenes require careful choreography because there's generally a lot of activity happening at once. Yet one advantage of these scenes is that crowd control is not a problem. The crime scene tape that we set up keeps curious onlookers at bay. And, indeed, if the public does stop to stare, it only enhances the air of authenticity.

In order to find a way to make the discovery of "Oxymoron's" dead body completely believable, during prep Director Gus Makris tested various ideas by doing a walk-through at the crime scene location. Second AD Luis Nieves and I acted out the crime scene roles. (I got to play the dead woman.) Gus was able to work out a way in which to obscure the body, yet balance that with enough elbowroom for the actors and the camera crew to work. Thanks to the thorough preparation, the shoot went smoothly, the body got up and went home, and we moved on to the next scene.

CASTING DIRECTOR: PRINCIPAL ACTORS

Suzanne Ryan, of Lynn Kressel Casting, is Law & Order's *four-time Emmy Award–nominated casting director, and has been with the show for thirteen seasons. Ryan casts the principal actors for each episode—all those who have speaking parts. Ryan's department includes Claire Traeger, her casting associate.*

Suzanne Ryan:

For every *Law & Order* episode, I do a character breakdown of the script, come up with ideas for the different roles, schedule the auditions, run the casting sessions, and negotiate the actors' deals. Although I have complete control over who gets in the door to audition, the final casting decisions are made in concert with the producer and the director. Having worked together for so long, however, we're usually in sync.

Casting for the crime scenes generally involves no more than seven or eight people. Although the dead body, as an "extra," is selected through background casting, I do cast the people who discover the body, as well as any other speaking roles in the Teaser's two scenes. In truth, casting the Aftermath scene is somewhat formulaic—typically involving a Crime Scene Unit (CSU), an assistant medical examiner (ME), possibly a uniformed officer (Uni), and perhaps a couple of witnesses. For two reasons, actors who play CSU personnel and MEs reappear on various episodes. The first reason is that these particular roles are, from episode to episode, basically routine and require a consistent delivery. No less important in casting these parts is the fact that, in terms of realism, it makes sense. In New York City, there are

actually only a limited number of people who do the jobs of the CSUs and the MEs. Conversely, I always cast different people as Unis, since, in actuality, there are many uniformed officers in the city.

There's an interesting aspect to casting the "civilians" who discover the body in the Teaser. It's difficult to find actors who are willing to play these parts. Most of the better actors refuse to do what generally amounts to two lines, opting, instead for roles that call for two pages. The fact is that it is much more challenging to take two lines and make them sound real. It's a good indicator of talent. For the "Oxymoron" crime scene, I cast two young women who fit the bill perfectly. I think they did a great job.

As a New York–based show, we do not have the same access to the large number of actors available to the television shows shot in Los Angeles. But, what we do have is special: a theater-based talent pool. We draw a tremendous number of people from the New York Theater venue and I'm truly thankful that they're here.

BACKGROUND CASTING

Fleet Emerson of Sylvia Fay Casting has been Law & Order's *background or "extras" casting director since the show's pilot. The background actors are the denizens of the streets and various interior locations, and of the* Law & Order *stages' police precinct, DA's offices, and courtroom. What defines the "extras" is that they never speak on film. They fill the background and create an atmosphere. With rare exception, the dead body is part of background casting.*

Fleet Emerson:

Of all the background roles on *Law & Order,* the most coveted is that of the dead body. Each season, I receive hundreds of inquiries from around the country from people who want to play dead. As sympathetic as I may feel, I have to deal with the realities of the business. By union contract, the dead body must be a member of the Screen Actors Guild. Sylvia Fay has a computerized database of approximately 8,000 SAG actors, filed by age, ethnicity, height, weight, hair color, skin type, and any unusual physical characteristics.

Despite its popularity with actors, playing *Law & Order's* dead body has one major drawback. Unlike other "extra" parts, where one person may play several background roles in one episode alone, the dead body cannot work on *Law & Order,* in any role, for at least one year after his or her initial appearance. It would not be smart to have someone who is dead in one episode appear in the next, casually strolling past Jerry Orbach. Of course, this rule was instituted before anyone imagined the possibility that the

show would have several daily reruns. I'm fairly certain that the ardent fans of the reruns have, on numerous occasions, witnessed an actor walking around, whom they have recently seen play dead. Given *Law & Order's* success, however, it's a circumstance that we can live with.

The script for "Oxymoron" arrived eight days before the shoot was to begin. The choice for the dead body was a bit tricky because the crime scene description of the victim was deliberately ambiguous. In the first version of the script, the body was found lying dead in the street, wearing a red teddy, suggesting that she was, perhaps, a hooker. (She turns out to be a doctor.) Thus, I needed to cast someone who, at first glance, could appear to be a prostitute, yet, as the story unfolded, could also be accepted by the audience as someone who was well bred and complicated. I chose four young women, to whom I explained the details of the crime scene and the morgue shots. They were all delighted to be in the running. Unlike our usual procedure, which is to first send the director their headshots, I opted to have the actresses go directly for interviews. I felt that the choice was for their entire presence. As it turned out, the crime scene was changed—the red teddy morphed into a black leather skirt with a sweater and a cashmere coat. The chosen actress was still correct for the role, and the body looked great on screen.

THE DEAD BODY

Amy Dorris played the dead body for the "Oxymoron" episode. A former model, Dorris has been studying acting in New York City.

Amy Dorris:

This was my first acting job for *Law & Order*, although I have worked on two other Dick Wolf productions—each time as a dead body. I'm not sure why it is that directors keep casting me to play dead. But whatever the reason, my stint as the dead body on *Law & Order* was by far the most exciting. The fact is that most actors whom I know would *die* for the part.

My audition was very simple. There were four of us in contention. The first and the second ADs gave a brief synopsis of the episode and further explained what was needed for the morgue and crime scene shoots. I was prepared to lie down to act out the scene, but it never happened. The director appeared, selected me, and I was whisked into costume design for a fitting for my crime scene outfit. The next day, after makeup was applied, I did a still photo shoot on the morgue set, which is a creepy place to be because it's so realistic. I also did a scene on film in the morgue, but all that was seen of me was my big toe with a tag attached.

At the crime scene shoot, there was an actress who had been selected to be my "lie-in." While the crew is setting up the scene, the lie-in is the person who plays the person who plays dead. The idea is to give the actor who is playing dead on screen a break or, to put it simply, to keep the body fresh. Because I felt that I needed time to adjust to my situation, I opted to lie on the street throughout. It was amusing when people passing by didn't

realize that we were filming. When they saw me practically lying under a car, they panicked. I had to keep reassuring people that I was fine.

THE COSTUME DESIGNER

Jennifer Von Mayrhauser, Law & Order's *Emmy Award–nominated costume designer, has been with the show for eleven seasons. Von Mayrhauser's staff consists of two full-time assistant costume designers, two full-time wardrobe supervisors, one part-time and two full-time wardrobe assistants, as well as a part-time tailor.*

Jennifer Von Mayrhauser:

The key to designing is to have a grasp of each character's identity. Essentially, I'm painting a portrait of the characters. I consider it my job to help the actors develop their roles. Although I get general ideas from the script and the director, I work directly with the actors to come up with what is most appropriate to their parts. It's important that they be comfortable, because, in my experience, if the clothes make sense, an actor's performance will be better. I'm also very aware of the use of color; I follow a particular palette to create an accent or to make a statement. The simple use of a certain color in a tie or in a pair of earrings, for example, can immediately tell you something about that person.

In the crime scenes, although sometimes the clothing on the dead body is meant to be ambiguous, most often it is the visual clue to the background of that character. And that's the setup for the entire story. It tells the viewer if the character is rich or poor,

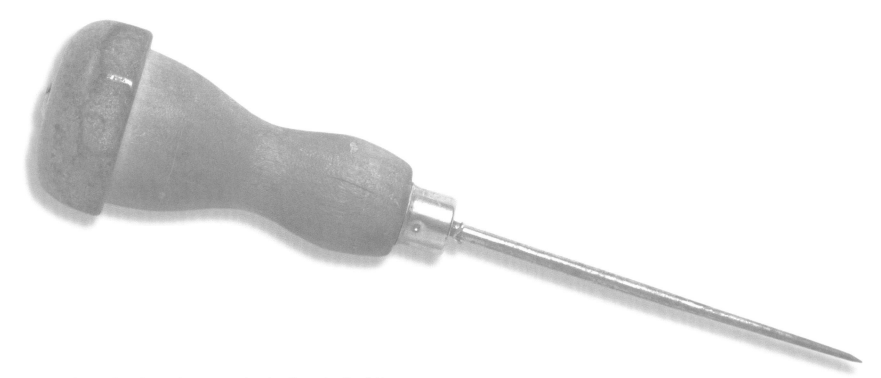

blue or white collar, homeless, etc. In the first draft of the "Oxymoron" script, the dead body was to be found dressed in a red teddy. By the time the actress was cast for the part, however, a script change called for more conservative clothing—a leather mini skirt, a simple top, a cashmere coat, chic heels, and expensive jewelry. Thus, the character's background was clearly established. At the fitting, I put our dead body, Amy Dorris, in a variety of tops and we selected one that she particularly liked and that suited the character and her backstory. We chose a cashmere coat in black, which was unusual because the use of black clothing can obscure the blood at a crime scene. Indeed, in costuming the dead bodies, I always have to think about whether the body has been shot or stabbed and how much blood there may eventually be. However, "Oxymoron" was not a bloody crime scene. With the director's input, I added a tear in her stockings and on set we added more rings to her fingers. At the scene, Michael Fisher, my wardrobe supervisor, worked on the stockinged leg, as Sharon Ilson, the make-up supervisor, created the leg wound. All told, I was very pleased by the results.

THE MAKE-UP SUPERVISOR

Sharon Ilson has been Law & Order's *make-up supervisor for three seasons. She studied Fine Arts at Sarah Lawrence College and was a painter before an eighteen-year career as a make-up artist on feature films. Apart from doing the makeup for the principal actors, the job of the make-up supervisor requires significant skills in creating special effects. Ilson is supported in her work by Make-up Artist Ruth Pontious.*

Sharon Ilson:

For every *Law & Order* crime scene, preparation and details are critical. I first find out what the director would like to see, ascertain how the injuries that caused the victim's death were sustained, and then research the appropriate wounds. *Law & Order* tends to be subtle in what it shows of the dead body on-screen, so the impact, though quick, must read dramatically.

The "Oxymoron" crime scene was an interesting one for me because it went through various makeup changes from the undetermined source of the ligature wound on the victim's neck to the supposed "mucus" coming from her nose, and, finally, the "road rash" on her leg. As rewrites of the script occurred, I continuously checked my pathology books, had discussions with the producer and the art director, and accessed a trusted site on the Web to make certain that every detail was correct. As I often do with the victims, I created the facial makeup twice—once for the morgue shots and then, again, for the crime scene. On location, I spent most of my time working on the leg wound of the victim. I had to try to imagine what a wound would look like if one were thrown from a car, as the dead body supposedly had been. Although the director had an idea of what would "read" on camera, I needed to get every detail right.

Ruth Pontious:

While Sharon Ilson works on the dead body, my contribution to the show's crime scenes is to touch up Detectives Briscoe and Green (Jerry Orbach and Jesse Martin), as well as all of the principal day players, such as the medical examiners, police officers, and witnesses. After completing the crime scene, we walk the dead body to the makeup truck to clean off the special effects— the bullet and/or knife wounds, the bruises, blood, etc. Often the "victim" is really a mess, with dripping blood, gashes to the head and the like. What's really extraordinary is to see the general public's reaction to the wounds. While many rush over with offers of help, others take absolutely no notice.

THE HAIR DEPARTMENT

Sandy Deblasio, the hair supervisor, has been working for Law & Order *for eight seasons. Robert Fama, the hair stylist, has three seasons to his credit.*

Sandy Deblasio and Robert Fama:

Between us, we have attended 154 *Law & Order* crime scenes. Many factors need to be taken into account when working on the hair of the dead body. First, of course, is the sex and age of the person. But we also have to adjust to whether the victim was rich or poor, funky or conservative, and where he or she was going to or coming from. The worst nightmare for our team is when a deadly blow causes a bloody mess in the hair and beyond the hairline. To maintain continuity between camera takes, we must be extremely vigilant about the placement of the hair locks. Care must be taken to ensure that the body never looks as if it has been moved. It's amazing how the audience picks up on the slightest lapse.

On "Oxymoron," we were blessed with a very well-behaved dead body. We did her hair only once. The actress never moved between takes which was unusual, unexpected, and a very pleasant surprise.

THE DIRECTOR OF PHOTOGRAPHY

John Beymer has been Law & Order's *director of photography (DP) for three seasons. The director of photography, also known as the cinematographer, heads the camera department and is the key person responsible for lighting. The cinematographer must take the director's vision and translate to the lighting crew exactly what he needs—all the while making certain that the camera shots coincide.*

John Beymer:

I approach any given set or action by first considering which compositions and lighting will enhance the director's vision of the scene. I want to tell the story without the camera being intrusive. With the director, I plan every move and how it will affect the lighting. I consider two factors: first, the possibilities offered by the set and the actors and, second, the possibilities offered by the mood outlined by the director—i.e., do I use my "happy" or "sad" lights? In using this method, it is essential to have a sympathetic director—one who is not averse to making occasional, slight changes in his action to improve the visual quality of the scene.

I find lighting for the crime scenes very interesting, particularly if they are at night or in the shadows of some interior. For me, the trick is to light the victim subtly, so that the body (or the wound) will not visually overpower the scene.

Because we were not lighting for the "Oxymoron" crime scene, in truth, what we really needed was luck. The scene was written for early morning and we began shooting just after dawn in the soft shadows of a tree-lined Upper West Side street. Although the brownstone buildings kept the harsh sunlight at bay, I was fighting

its growing emergence in the distance. We finished the last shot within moments of its appearance. Luck was with us, and the timing worked out perfectly.

SHOOTING STILLS OF THE CRIME SCENE

Jessica Burstein has been Law & Order's *still photographer for nine seasons. The work of the still photographer includes shooting the cast title shots, advertising and publicity photographs for newspapers and magazines, and the "evidence" stills that appear on the show.*

Jessica Burstein:

Looking back through my early *Law & Order* crime scene stills, they now appear to me as virtual shots in the dark. This was before I began to do research, including studying crime scene photographs, having discussions with the police, and, most sobering of all, visiting real crime scenes. But, no matter how much research I have done and how much I have learned, the work is a constant challenge because of the reality of the situation—that I am shooting illusions. As someone who was drawn to photography as a means of revealing truths, it is strange, indeed, to have spent so much time doing precisely the opposite.

When taken out of the context of *Law & Order,* the crime scene photographs have generated reactions ranging from perverse fascination to genuine horror. The most astonishing reaction came from four seasoned New York City homicide detectives who, when shown some photographs without explanation, began to argue with

each other about who of them had been at which crime scene. Although I was surprised by their response, it would be disingenuous of me to claim that I was not pleased by it.

Shooting the *Law & Order* crime scenes requires meeting the demands of the show's filming schedule. I don't always have dedicated time in which to do my work and often have to photograph the scene between camera takes, trying to avoid catching the crew or equipment in the shot. In achieving what I believe will work for the stills, the job requires timing, speed, and the need to connect with the actor playing dead. The actors—often barely dressed and lying in unpleasant places—tend to be extraordinarily cooperative. I'm continuously surprised at the reaction of the general public when passing by a crime scene location. Despite the fact that it's clearly a *Law & Order* film crew working, I'm constantly asked, "Who died?"

I had worked with our "Oxymoron" dead body, Amy Dorris, twice before on other Dick Wolf productions. Because she's an old hand at playing dead, technically, the shoot went smoothly. However, I felt that the "Oxymoron" crime scene did not translate particularly well for the still photography. Unless the scene's design is very graphic, in stills, the daylight crime scene can appear to be flat. As much as I try to bring reality to illusion, I primarily succeed when the atmosphere is more controlled or disguised. Thus, I am partial to the *Law & Order* night exterior crime scenes for their inherent darkness. And, of course, nighttime crime scenes play into our imaginations. I think that, ultimately, what I am after is, in fact, an oxymoron: a beautiful crime scene.

MOMENTS IN THE MORGUE:
Depending upon the episode, I shoot morgue photographs that are used on *Law & Order* generally for the purpose of victim identification. The morgue set is frighteningly realistic and has been witness to some of the more bizarre moments in my work. Upon entering the set, the actors, understandably nervous, sometimes respond with strange behavior. A nine-year-old girl, fully made-up with bloody gunshot wounds to her head, sat on the morgue table and insisted on singing all of "God Bless America"—*twice.*
I had a very difficult time shooting photographs of a man who could not stop laughing. It turned out that his sense of humor had been honed in the New York City morgue, where he'd worked as a cleaner for the previous eighteen years.
The most frightening moment belonged to an elderly man, who immediately upon lying down on the morgue table, fell asleep. I was happy about this until the shoot was over and I tried to awaken him. For what seemed like an eternity, but was probably no more than a minute, the art director and I were yelling his name. Receiving no response, I lifted his arm to feel for a pulse, when he suddenly jumped up, wide-awake. Needless to say, there was great relief all around.

THE PROPERTY MASTER

Ron Stone, Law & Order's *prop master (as the job is familiarly termed), is one of the original crew members, having started with the series' pilot in 1990. Stone left the show for a four-year stint in feature films, returning in 1999. The job of the prop master is to supply any object an actor touches or works with—from large vehicles to a tiny pencil. As well, all special effects fall under the aegis of his department. Stone's support team consists of a full-time crew of three and an additional assistant on location days.*

Ron Stone:

Although there is a rhythm to my job, it is a constantly changing one. Since every episode of *Law & Order* is different, the props always vary. I'm continuously wrapping out the props from the previous episode, working on those for the present one, and preparing for the following episode. Unlike some shows where the prop master is rarely on set, I'm very hands-on because I want to be true to the director's vision. I'm extremely busy, but never more so than for the crime scenes.

The crime scenes are given the most production values. Apart from numerous vehicles that my department supplies—fire trucks, ambulances, police cars, civilian cars, and the like—we have to prop every person who appears in the scene, from the principal actors to all the extras. Our *Law & Order* "detectives" have their designated holsters, guns, and badges. For the extras playing police officers, I supply fully stocked gun belts, as well as guns (all fakes), handcuffs, flashlights, etc. They're each given badges, with nameplates and merit bars (also all fakes). Crime scene

tape is always used and we hand out rubber gloves to everyone. If there's a medical examiner, I have to prop the person with a stethoscope, a doctor's bag, and a crime scene kit. Almost everyone has an ID badge of some sort and has something in hand that we've supplied. From evidence bags to body bags, the prop department is *Law & Order's* virtual shop. However, when the crime scene shoot concludes, we're extremely vigilant, for obvious reasons, about the return of all the items.

On "Oxymoron," the work was fairly standard. I supplied six vehicles, propped thirty extras, and, in addition to Jerry and Jesse, three principal actors. But, despite the added workload, I prefer more complicated crime scenes, especially those filmed at night. To polish the look of a scene, I'll often perform a "wetdown" of the street or add a "bubble" light bar, enhancing the lights from the tops of the police cars. I am constantly creating illusions because, in fact, on film, reality does not always feel real. Yet, in New York City, where just about anything can happen, I've had many moments in my job where illusion and reality meet. Among these moments was one that occurred in a West Village building. While propping a *Law & Order* crime scene, suddenly, real police officers came running in. Apparently, there had actually been a crime committed on another floor. Unprepared, an officer sheepishly asked: "Would it be possible to borrow some crime scene tape?"

THE GRIP DEPARTMENT

Carl Peterson has been Law & Order's *key grip for eleven seasons. Jeremy Schroeder has worked on the show for seven seasons, the last six as the second man in charge, known as the best boy grip. The department's core group consists of five men, with an additional five working on heavy days. The grip department is one-half of the lighting crew. It is responsible for on-set rigging and construction, as well as the camera dolly moves and on-set safety.*

Carl Peterson and Jeremy Schroeder:

For the grip department, the "Oxymoron" crime scene was very simple. Since it was shot in natural daylight, there was no construction and no rigging necessary. We set up one large reflector to pick up some light and one "flag" to control flare. Our dolly grip, Miles Strassner, was, as usual, backing up the camera crew.

Although daylight crime scenes, like that of "Oxymoron" give us a break in a really grueling schedule, we much prefer to work on the crime scenes that are night exteriors. For these scenes, our department plays a big part. We help the electricians by rigging powerful lights onto rooftops or cranes and hoisting them high above the streets. We often light up several city blocks. It's hard work, but there's something really special about looking down the street on a nice New York night and seeing a few blocks of the city that we've lit up.

THE GAFFER

William Klayer, Law & Order's *gaffer (the chief lighting technician), has been with the show for twelve seasons. Since season eleven, his duties also include work as the second unit director of photography. There's a core group of five electricians on staff.*

William Klayer:

Because of the look of *Law & Order*, we do not light a day exterior, as is done on feature films. During the time that the crew is shooting an exterior scene, as occurred with "Oxymoron," I am usually at an interior location pre-lighting a scene that will be shot later that day. Still, for "Oxymoron," I scouted the crime scene location in advance of the shoot and made blocking suggestions based on the available light.

For night crime scenes, my preparations are very extensive and lighting considerations are a key element in staging the scenes. At the tech scout, I work with the director to get specific descriptions of the shots. I then determine the equipment needs, create a basic lighting plot and coordinate it with Best Boy Patrick Cousins, and with our key grip, Carl Peterson. When possible, we have a crew pre-lighting night scenes. On one occasion, I sent a crew to pre-light a riverfront crime scene. They had to wait. The police were pulling a real body out of the Hudson.

THE SOUND MIXER

Richard Murphy, CSA (Cinema Audio Society), an Emmy Award nominee, worked as Law & Order's *sound mixer for three seasons. Technically, the job of the sound mixer involves recording the show's dialogue in the most expeditious manner—i.e., with minimal looping (dialogue replacement) requirements. There are two full-time sound assistants. (Richard Murphy left the show after season twelve and was replaced by Larry Hoff.)*

Richard Murphy:

Law & Order, as a story driven show, is very dialogue oriented. In consequence, the sound has to compliment all the nuances that make *Law & Order* so special. When we shoot at the stages, the work, though not easy, is more controlled, as we're familiar with the permanent sets and there are built-in sound barriers. Locations, however, are a whole other matter. Since the *Law & Order* crime scenes are invariably location shoots, we have to contend with a wide range of challenges.

New York City is a cacophony of random sounds. To the point of ignoring them, most New Yorkers eventually adjust to the levels. But, on any given day, were you to actually key into the sounds, it's really quite extraordinary. There's sound from vehicular traffic, pedestrian traffic, sanitation trucks, helicopters, planes, boats, subways, street drilling, construction, street music, objects being moved, arguments, pigeon calls, barking dogs, police and fire sirens, etc. Thus, when shooting at exterior locations, as was the case with the "Oxymoron" crime scene, there's a saying among the sound mixers in the New York film industry: "We live by our wits and our mikes." On *Law & Order,* to diminish the level of the background noise, we generally use radio microphones. The mikes are placed very close to the actors' mouths, so that the dialogue will be clear. Should a loud sound interfere with the actors' dialogue, I do a pick-up of the lost dialogue on a "wild track." The dialogue is re-recorded at the actors' original spot so that the background ambience will match the rest of the track. It is then reintroduced with the film footage in post-production.

"Oxymoron" was my sixtieth *Law & Order* crime scene and from a technical standpoint was not particularly difficult. We used two radio mikes and a boom for ambience. From an audio point of view, conceptually this crime scene was interesting because the sound emphasized the inherent contrast of the scene. It was an unusually quiet morning, and one could clearly hear the sound of the breeze, the chirping of birds, and children laughing. These tranquil sounds created an illusion of peacefulness. Thus, by the time the camera showed the dead body, there was greater impact and the illusion was complete.

THE SCRIPT SUPERVISOR

Cynthia Balfour has been Law & Order's *script supervisor for six seasons. Because of the intensity of the job, most one-hour television dramas have supervisors who alternate episodes. Balfour, however, singly handles the work.*

Cynthia Balfour:

The essence of my job is, literally, timing, and over the course of six years on *Law & Order*, I've had to develop the ability to juggle. I always have varying elements up in the air, because while I'm on set for one episode, I'm simultaneously prepping for the next.

Prepping an episode involves pre-timing the script. This means that I have to estimate how long each scene will end up lasting on screen, imagine how fast the actors are going to speak, find out the area in which they will act, and have a sense of what the director is planning to do. With each script revision, I have to revise the timing. Along with the assistant directors, I plan out the shooting days. We decide when one day ends and another logically begins. I then tell the costume department, for example, how many changes they will need. I also have to decide how much time elapses from scene to scene. If there's a scene that's scripted to air contiguously with another, but the two are being shot a week apart, I need to pay special attention to the flow and the look, and to help the actors.

The crime scenes require attention to minute details and everything has to be double-checked. As an example, in the script, there are often scenes in the morgue where references are made to something that was "visible" at the crime scene. Yet, the scripted crime scene may have made no mention of this and no matter how subtle the reference, I obviously have to note and follow up on it. In addition, since the Teaser consists of two scenes, the dead body, as well as any other players, must look exactly the same in both. After one scene is shot, Polaroids are taken of the placement of the body, the hair, the makeup, and the wardrobe. This is critical should the dead body get up to take a break between the scenes. The people who've discovered the body also have to precisely match from scene to scene. Fortunately, I can always count on the hair, makeup, and wardrobe crew to be on top of potential problems.

For the "Oxymoron" crime scene, some script changes were made at the location. There was a reference to an injury to the dead body's arm and shoulder, which, because she was in a coat, made no sense and was taken out. Also, because of the angle from which Gus, the director, wanted to shoot, the wound was changed on set from the right to the left leg. I had to remind an actor to say "left" side, because he'd memorized "right." On the whole, "Oxymoron's" crime scene was easier for me than some others because there was barely any blood and, in consequence, less to worry about for matching.

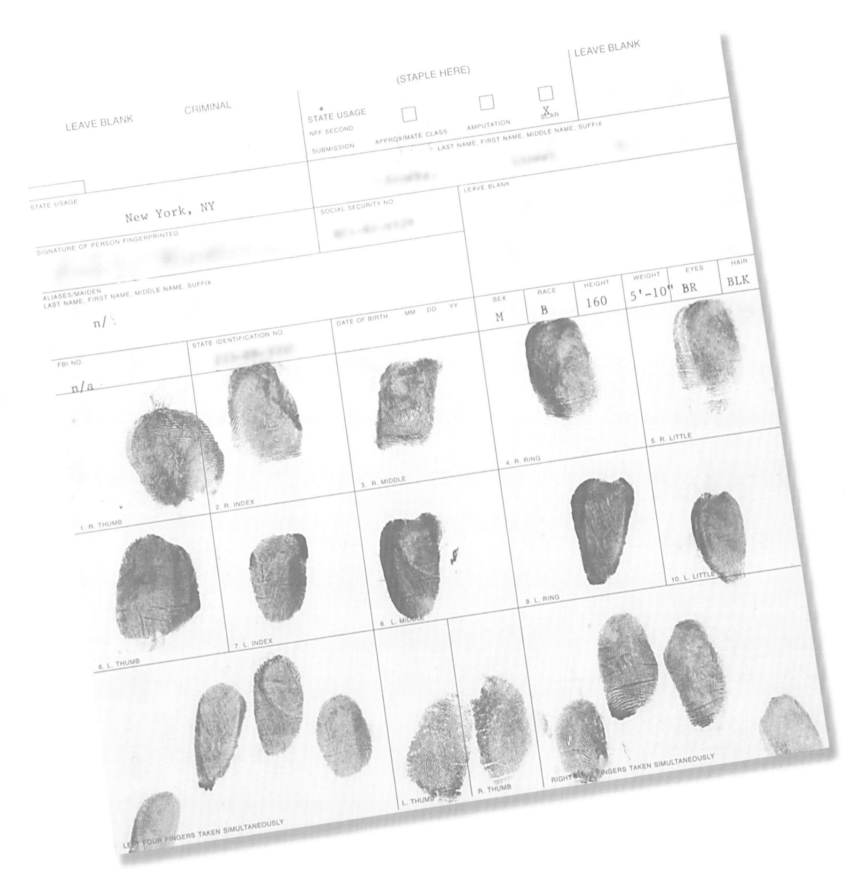

LEAVE BLANK   CRIMINAL

(STAPLE HERE)

LEAVE BLANK

STATE USAGE

NFF SECOND
SUBMISSION

☐ APPROXIMATE CLASS   ☐ AMPUTATION   ☒ SCAR

LAST NAME, FIRST NAME, MIDDLE NAME, SUFFIX

STATE USAGE

New York, NY

SOCIAL SECURITY NO

LEAVE BLANK

SIGNATURE OF PERSON FINGERPRINTED

ALIASES/MAIDEN
LAST NAME, FIRST NAME, MIDDLE NAME, SUFFIX

n/a

FBI NO.

n/a

			SEX	RACE	HEIGHT	WEIGHT	EYES	HAIR
	DATE OF BIRTH MM DD YY		M	B	160	5'-10"	BR	BLK

STATE IDENTIFICATION NO.

1. R. THUMB
2. R. INDEX
3. R. MIDDLE
4. R. RING
5. R. LITTLE

6. L. THUMB
7. L. INDEX
8. L. MIDDLE
9. L. RING
10. L. LITTLE

LEFT FOUR FINGERS TAKEN SIMULTANEOUSLY

L. THUMB

R. THUMB

RIGHT FOUR FINGERS TAKEN SIMULTANEOUSLY

PG #: 47

ABOUT THE NYPD MOVIE/TV UNIT

The NYPD Movie/TV Unit was established in 1966, with the inception of the Mayor's Office of Film, Theatre & Broadcasting. The Unit is a part of the Traffic Control Division (the TCD), the large police bureau that oversees everything dealing with transportation in New York City. A free service provided to the entertainment industry by the city of New York, the NYPD Movie/TV Unit consists of one lieutenant, four sergeants, and twenty-five police officers. Admission to this highly coveted assignment is extremely difficult. In December 2002, Lieutenant Jay Fagan became the head of the Unit. Fagan replaced John Battista, who had been the Unit's lieutenant for a little more than three years and is presently the deputy commissioner at the Mayor's Office of Film, Theatre & Broadcasting.

John Battista:

Our primary goal is to ensure public safety at exterior movie and television locations, as well as to control the flow of vehicular and pedestrian traffic at these sites. Prior to filming, the locations aspect of each script is combed through, scene by scene, to avoid any potential safety or traffic problems. The Unit's lieutenant attends production meetings and all location scouts. As the Movie/TV Unit's lieutenant, every day I visited exterior locations for every production shooting in New York. I made sure that each officer had checked that the production was in compliance with the Schedule A (legal parking clearance), and had verified child permits, inspected water usage sources and permits, ensured that all firearms on set were inoperable, and negotiated any number of

circumstances that could turn into possible safety issues.

Anytime there is a production that involves a number of actors playing police officers, the Unit enforces very strict regulations. The single most important one is that when leaving a set, even momentarily, any actor dressed as a police officer must cover up the uniform. The actor could conceivably walk into a dangerous situation, be mistaken for a police officer, and end up in harm's way. We also have to avoid confusion on set between "real" officers and actors. The tip-off is the collar brass. On any film or television production, it is forbidden to use the number of any existing New York City police precinct. *Law & Order,* for example, uses the fictitious 27th Precinct. Thus, if that number is on the collar brass, it tells you that the "officer" is really an actor.

As the Deputy Commissioner of Film, Theatre & Broadcasting, I still visit sets and I encourage production to come into our great city. But, I have to say this: *Law & Order* has always been a pleasure to work with. It has been shooting here for a long time and knows exactly what, where, and how to do it.

THE TEAMSTER CAPTAIN

Bill Curry has been Law & Order's *Teamster captain, the key person in charge of transportation, for thirteen seasons. Curry oversees a crew of sixteen drivers.*

Bill Curry:

The Teamsters drive the equipment trucks for each of *Law & Order*'s departments, as well as the motor homes, makeup and hair trailer, wardrobe trailer, set dressing truck, crew vans, and the cars that pick up the actors. We're the first on set and the last to leave. The reality is that if the camera, grip, or electric equipment trucks are late or break down, it can completely halt production.

Every crime scene begins, for my department, days before its actual scheduled day. There are generally many set dressing items that have to be picked up in advance. On the day of the crime scene, we deliver the set dressing, the picture cars, and the props to the crew for setup and pick them up after breakdown. Probably the most unusual aspect of the "Oxymoron" shoot was that the call time required us to arrive extra early—at an hour, where for some night shoots, we would have been wrapping, not arriving.

Our job does involve some sensitivity to public relations. Let's face it, a good legal parking spot in New York City is golden. So when people drive by, looking to park, and all the spots for a few blocks are taken . . . well, let's just say there's a bit of grumbling. We do try our best to be accommodating, however. (Usually, it's to tell them, nicely, to look elsewhere.)

THE ESTIMATOR

Susan Hayes is an accountant who has been Law & Order's *estimator for three seasons. Her job is to budget each episode, department by department, track the costs of each episode from the first day of shooting through post-production, and issue reports that are distributed to the producers and the studio.*

Susan Hayes:

The crime scenes are usually the most involved part of the discussions at the production meeting. And often they're the most costly scenes in an episode. The department heads let me know the scope of the crime scene and what I should include in the budget. For the crime scene in "Oxymoron," I budgeted for the following:

Picture cars—one ambulance, one Crime Scene Unit wagon, one patrol car, and three additional vehicles.

Extras—thirty background players: one dead body, a five-person Crime Scene Unit, five uniformed police officers, two EMS workers, fifteen onlookers, and two stand-ins.

The dead body, an extra, was paid more than scale, receiving $111.00 plus a $50.00 "bump" for a total of $161.00. The "bump" was given as a bonus because the actress was particularly accommodating in playing dead.

DETECTIVE ED GREEN

Jesse L. Martin, who plays Detective Ed Green, joined the cast of Law & Order *in its tenth season. To learn more about Detective Green, see page 128.*

Jesse L. Martin

For every crime scene, what is most important is how much information I get. I want to have every detail so that I can play every note. As an actor, the most interesting facet of the crime scene is that it's filmed in one shot. It's particularly challenging to catch the moment, working in harmony with the dialogue, the visuals, the sound, and all the other elements that make up the scene.

Working with Jerry Orbach is a gift. Jerry's an extraordinary and generous actor. And he's got a photographic memory. Even if the dialogue is changed at the very last minute, he not only instantaneously knows his lines, he knows mine. In fact, he knows *everybody's.* I can always count on him. When I joined the cast, I was terrified. I suddenly found myself working with Jerry—an icon in an iconic show. I was shaking when I walked into my first scene, which was with Jerry and another hard-core pro, Epatha (S. Epatha Merkerson). Within minutes of working, Jerry and Epatha had shrunk the space in the room to just the three of us and I hit all the points that were needed for the scene. I cannot describe what a relief that was.

The character of Ed Green is written as being more openly emotional than that of Jerry's character, Lennie Briscoe. So, our approach to the crime scenes differs. The first thing I do at the crime scene is to meet the actor who plays the dead body and to ask if he or she is okay. Apart from being a simple act of courtesy, I know that any contact with the dead body seeps into Green. It was the seventh day of filming when we shot the "Oxymoron" crime scene and I'd imagined a whole history for the victim—a family, friends, etc. I made the person into an individual whom I carried with me throughout the episode. By the time we shot the scene, I couldn't get over the fact that the body was lying there "dead." On "Oxymoron," what got to me was how young the victim was and how senseless the murder. It's always more poignant when it's a young person who should not have been involved in that situation at all—in this case, because of drugs.

Acting in the scene went smoothly. We had very few takes and essentially they were caused by minor technical glitches. After three seasons on *Law & Order,* I still find the work really challenging, although I believe I've come a long way from the frightened guy who walked into that first scene. I feel truly blessed to have been given the opportunity to be a part of what I consider to be the Ivy League of television shows.

DETECTIVE LENNIE BRISCOE

Jerry Orbach, who portrays the case-hardened Detective Lennie Briscoe, joined the cast in season three. For an in-depth look at this character, see page 122.

Jerry Orbach:

A major reward for my work on *Law & Order* is the positive response that I receive from New York City police officers. They thank me for what they believe is a realistic portrayal of an NYPD detective. For an actor, that kind of acknowledgement is hard to beat.

Indeed, Briscoe, as written, is a real character—no pun intended. And he's a guy who has been around the block. He's had some rough times: a daughter killed by drug dealers, two divorces, and recovery from alcoholism. Still, after ten years of traipsing around in his shoes, there's always something new that I can bring to his character. It's a challenge that begins with the beginning of each script: the crime scene.

Coming upon the crime scene is the first moment of the case and it's where the detectives' experience, imagination, and logic kick in. It sets the tone for everything that follows and, as such, has to be as believable as possible. Since Briscoe has seen so much brutality in his years on the job, there's a certain balance of emotions required to make the crime scenes work from episode to episode. What I've tried to bring to the character is an affect that falls somewhere between being desensitized and being depressed—two emotional responses that, under real circumstances, would not be unusual. Briscoe covers his emotions with a

wry, often sardonic voice. And he's definitely given leeway because of his status as one of the old-timers, who has been there and seen it all. Indeed, Briscoe is a bit of a dinosaur in the police department, down to his gun, a .38 he insists on carrying, rather than the regulation Glocks issued to the younger officers.

The "Oxymoron" crime scene was pretty straightforward. The dialogue was not heavy and, as is most often the case for a day-time Teaser, the scene was done in one shot. In point of fact, "one-ers" are a breeze for me, 'cause I'm a one-take kind of a guy. In the scene, Jesse did the more physical work of squatting down over the body. Indeed, if viewers carefully watch any *Law & Order* Teaser, they'll notice that I never have to squat down. That's a perk for the "old timer." Jesse's a total professional and very generous, which I find to be the rule of thumb for actors who were trained in the theater. His character, Ed Green, is written to be more overtly emotional than mine and thus, with the crime scenes, we play off each other particularly well. With Green, there's an undercurrent of disbelief; with Briscoe, there's an undercurrent of disconnect.

I know that the fans pay special attention to each episode's Teaser because they're invariably quoting to me my throwaway, or cut, lines. I find it amusing. Truly, for an actor, I've got a dream job, from which I hope never to wake up and hear the throwaway line from the "Oxymoron" Teaser: "Dream's over."

DRESSING THE DEAD BODY

BLOCKING SCENE ONE

SHOOTING SCENE ONE

THE "COPS" ARRIVE

BLOCKING SCENE TWO

BEGIN SHOOTING SCENE TWO

COMPLETING THE SHOOTING OF SCENE TWO

THE CRIME SCENE WRAPS

SCENES OF THE CRIME

A NOTE ABOUT THE CRIME SCENES

The following *Law & Order* crime, morgue, and evidence shots
were photographed between 1994 and 2003. The avid and eagle-
eyed fan may be able to identify the episodes from which the
scenes were taken. For those less certain, however, one need only
visit the back section of the book, "Postmortem," to uncover
the details.

While looking at these photographs, it should be remembered
that for *Law & Order,* the crime scene is the necessary departure
point in the *why* of the crime and ultimately in the search for
justice. Great care has always been exercised in producing these
scenes, from the technical support of the New York City Police
Department and other law enforcement agencies to the immense
talent of the crew in translating, with integrity, the visual details
of a crime. These photographs are *representations* of violence,
which spares no age, no gender, no social stratum, and no ethnicity.

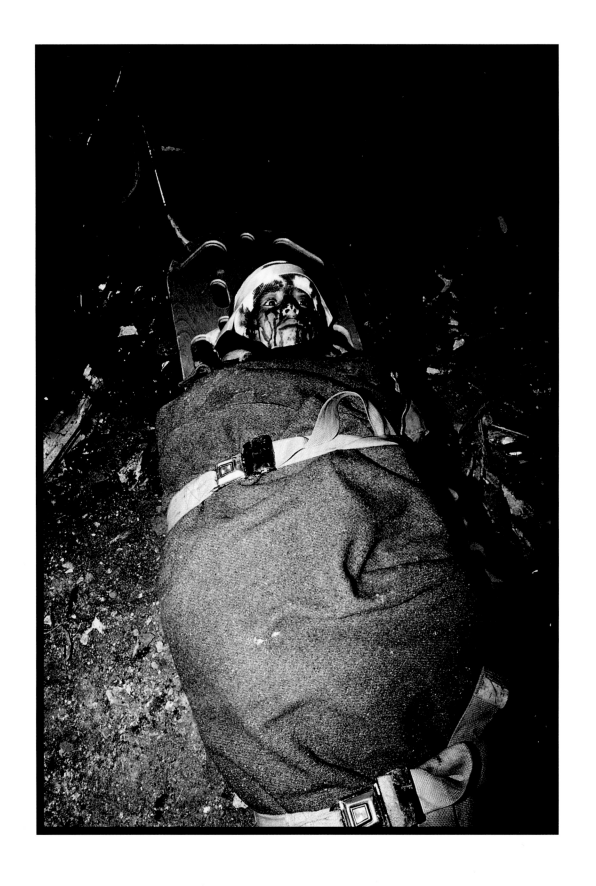

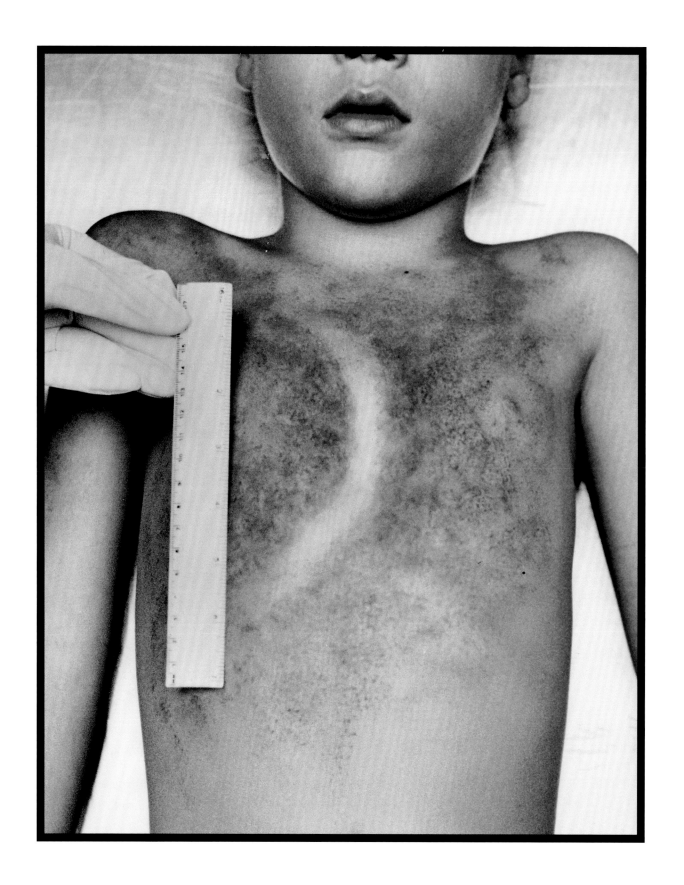

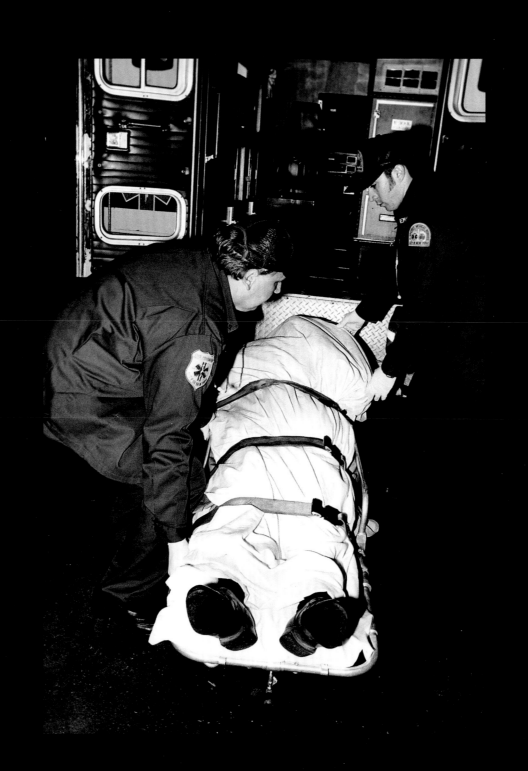

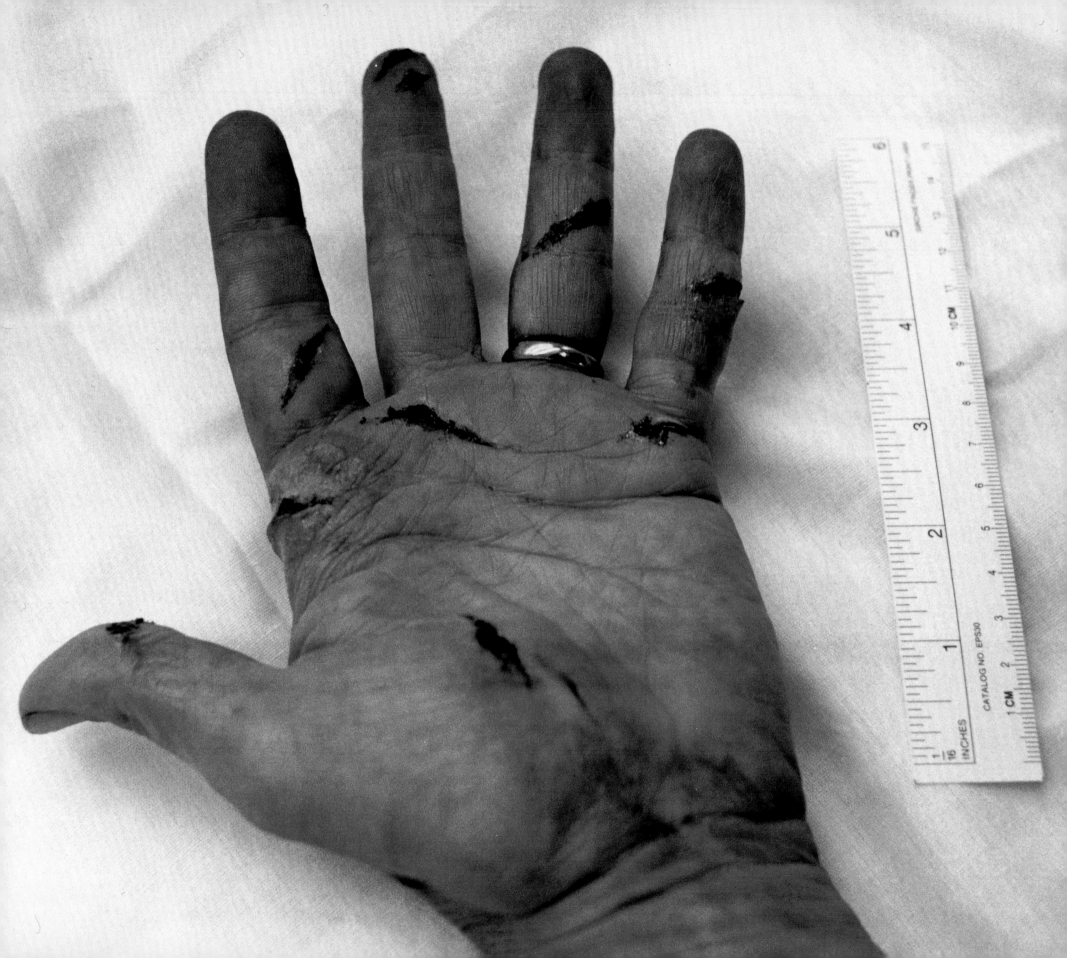

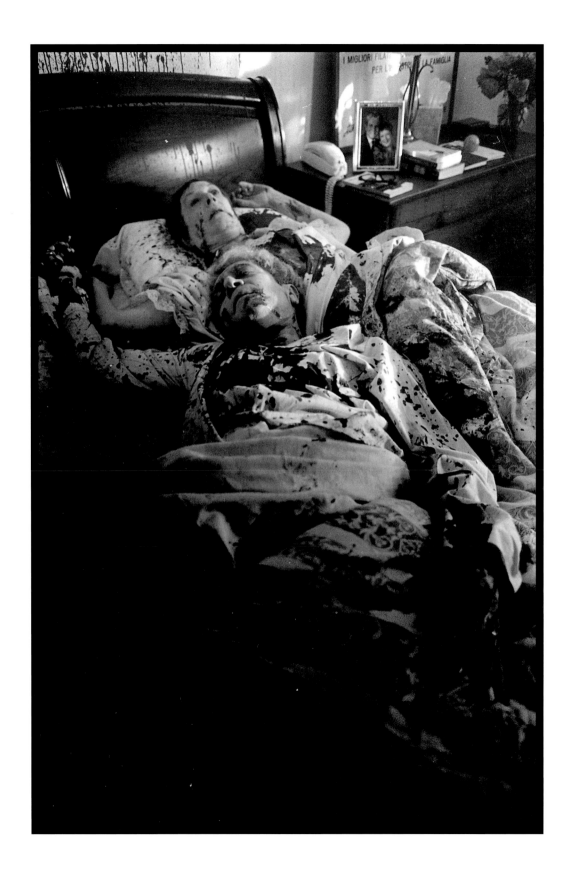

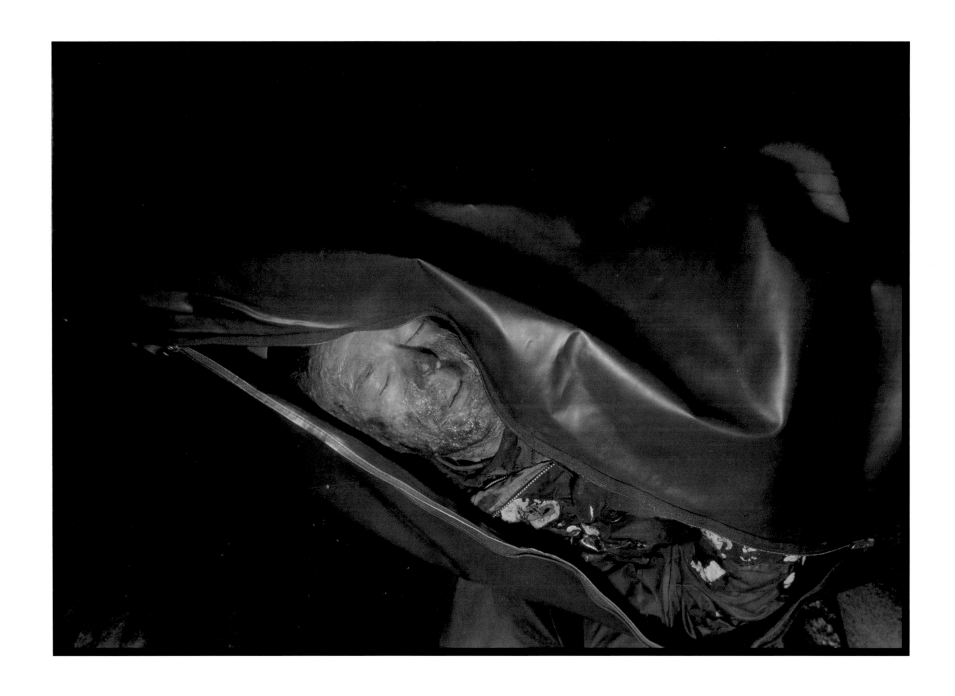

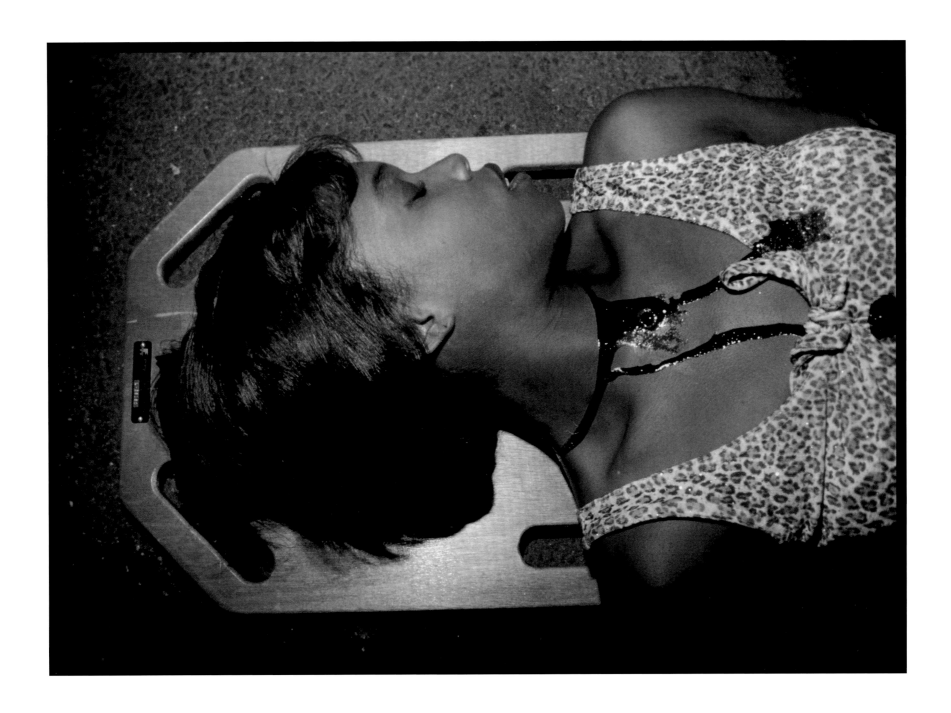

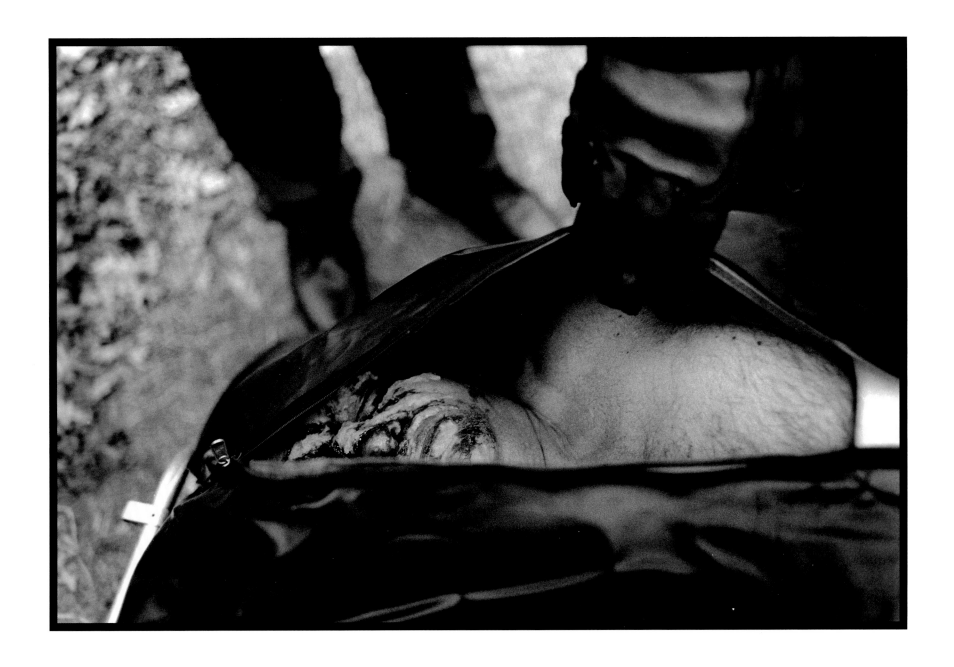

IN THE CRIMINAL JUSTICE SYSTEM

As the audience clearly knows, *Law & Order* is not a character-driven show. We do not go home with the characters and we do not focus on their personal lives. However, while the show focuses on the plot, the characters play a pivotal role—bringing their unique strengths, prejudices, and perspectives to each story line.

Therefore, when creating new characters, I have always considered how each could enrich the writing possibilities. I consult with the writers to get a general idea of what will inspire them, and try to create a fitting personality. In particular, with the partnerships that exist among the police and prosecutors, the writers have been able to expand the range of dramatic conflict by having personalities whose needs and reactions differ. In addition, and no less important, the actors who play these characters have been encouraged to bring whatever instincts they have to flesh out their alter egos. We listen very carefully to their opinions—if something does not ring true to them, we make the necessary changes. And one piece of inside information: in all of my shows, I choose the characters' first names very deliberately—those of my family and my friends.

Over the years, bits and pieces of the characters' backstories have slowly and subtly been revealed in varying amounts. As the show progressed and more characters came and went, the viewers became increasingly curious about these men and women whose lives we do not see. What follows is a personal look at each of the characters—their lives and the objectives behind their creations. *Law & Order*'s detectives and prosecutors represent varying interpretations of crime and justice. These are their stories.

MAX GREEVEY Detective Sergeant

Detective Sergeant Max Greevey, the working-class hero of *Law & Order* detectives, was born in the show's pilot, "Everybody's Favorite Bagman." But the audience did not officially meet him until the first-aired episode, "Prescription for Death," which debuted on September 13, 1990. (The pilot eventually aired later in the season.) As one of *Law & Order's* original characters, Greevey was emblematic of the spare style that I hoped would set the tone for the show.

In creating Max Greevey's character, I wanted him to represent the quintessential meat-and-potatoes cop with a no-nonsense view of his profession. He needed to look as if he'd been kicking around for awhile—a guy who had eaten a lot of doughnuts on the job and was shaped by his time in the department. My first choice for the role was George Dzundza, whom I had outfitted in plain, almost sloppy attire—from bad choices in ties to unattractive, albeit, sensible shoes. His style, in short, was no style.

I paired Max Greevey with Detective Mike Logan in order to create real opportunities for dramatic tension. Greevey was a devout Catholic, which allowed the writers to deepen the conflict with his more liberal (and lapsed Catholic) partner—as the two confronted complicated issues such as sexual "sin" and the bombing of an abortion clinic. They formed a "father-son" team of opposites: Logan was young and single; Greevey was mature and married, with three children. Where Logan's approach to the job was principally pragmatic, Greevey saw the bitter irony in life.

At the end of the first season, George Dzundza decided to leave the show. Thus, on September 17, 1991, Max Greevey, while working overtime, was gunned down and out of the scripts. Because I wanted him to have a send-off to match his "lunch box" roots, I had the writers give him a traditional, formal burial, with inspectors' honors. We added bagpipes and a military salute, and said good-bye to the most traditional cop ever to grace *Law & Order's* 27th Precinct.

GEORGE DZUNDZA AS DET. SGT. MAX GREEVEY (THE PILOT EPISODE AND SEASON ONE)

Along with his partner, Max Greevey, Detective Mike Logan was scripted into *Law & Order*'s pilot. Both detectives initially appeared to be fashioned from the same cloth— working-class Irish Catholic—but my final design revealed characters whose personalities vastly differed. I had found my idea for the mature, world-weary, deeply religious charac- ter of Max Greevey in George Dzundza. For the young, hotheaded, secular Mike Logan, I selected the very talented Chris Noth.

In developing the character of Logan, the only predictable element was his unpre- dictability—which gave the writers a lot of room in which to work. In his backstory, I made Mike Logan the son of physically abusive, alcoholic parents who had raised him as a strict Catholic and used religion as justification for punishment. To give more voice to his volatility, I added in the fact that as a boy, he had been sexually molested by a priest. Thus, Logan, badly damaged by his parents, also had severe disdain for what he per- ceived as the hypocrisy of the church. His resultant anger would haunt him throughout his career as a police officer.

On the job, Logan was not, on occasion, shy about using his fists. While he had a tra- ditional view of law and order, his rebellious nature precluded him from following police procedural rules when he felt his cause was just—which was often. Yet, Logan was capa- ble of showing real decency and he was extremely loyal to his partners, all three of whom eventually came to see him as a slightly wayward son.

By the end of season five, the writers felt that the pairing of Logan with his third part- ner, Lennie Briscoe, was too limiting, because their opinions closely matched. It was a difficult decision to make, but on May 24, 1995, in the episode "Pride," Mike Logan was transferred out of the 27th Precinct for having slugged a politician, and was demot- ed to walking a beat in Staten Island. The protests against his departure came in by the thousands and, to this day, Logan remains the most popular character ever to have appeared on *Law & Order*. In recognition of the fans' connection to Logan's bad-boy charm, I brought him back in *Exiled: A Law & Order Movie,* which aired in 1998.

CHRIS NOTH AS DET. MIKE LOGAN (THE PILOT EPISODE AND SEASONS ONE THROUGH FIVE)

DONALD CRAGEN Captain

Although the captain is the highest-ranking officer in the 27th Precinct, the role was not originally envisioned as a large one. With *Law & Order*'s Spartan scenes, it was necessary to give almost the entire first half of the show's airtime to the detectives investigating the crimes. Still, to realistically portray what occurs in a police precinct, it was essential to have a "boss" to whom the detectives report. I wanted an actor whose presence would fill the script in the way the actual pages did not. Thus, for the role of Captain Donald Cragen, I selected Dann Florek, a strong actor certain to leave an impression with the audience.

I gave Cragen an Irish Catholic background, a wife, Marge, and a teenaged child. Like Lennie Briscoe, he was a recovering alcoholic. Unlike most supervisory personnel, Cragen would have preferred to have loosened his tie and worked the cases himself. This was particularly evident at the end of the first season, when the writers finally took Cragen out of his office and put him into the hot seat to defend himself against the suspicion of corruption. Although in his backstory, Cragen was once partnered with Max Greevey, of all the detectives who came under his command—Greevey, Phil Cerreta, Mike Logan, and Briscoe—it was Logan with whom he had a special bond. This, in large part, reflected Dann Florek's close relationship with Chris Noth. Florek, at times frustrated with so little to do, used his personal preferences and improvisational moments to flesh out the character of Donald Cragen.

At the end of season three, with NBC insisting that I fill two of *Law & Order*'s roles with females, I made a decision to move Cragen out of the precinct. Although no script explained his disappearance, this was not to be the last that viewers saw of Donald Cragen. He returned for a guest appearance in the fifth season in the episode "Bad Faith" (which Florek directed, along with two earlier episodes) as head of the NYPD's Anti-Corruption Task Force. He later reappeared in *Exiled: A Law & Order Movie.* Presently, the caustic, witty Cragen is commanding the squad at *Law & Order: Special Victims Unit.*

DANN FLOREK AS CAPT. DONALD CRAGEN (THE PILOT EPISODE AND SEASONS ONE THROUGH THREE)

PHIL CERRETA Detective Sergeant

Detective Sergeant Phil Cerreta first appeared on *Law & Order* in the season two episode "Confession." In Phil Cerreta, I created the most joyful character we've had on *Law & Order*, one with a rich cultural background and a wonderful love of life. I envisioned him as the exact opposite of the tired, traditional police officer embodied by his predecessor, Max Greevey. With Cerreta, I sought to accomplish three things: a strong transition into a new character, an introduction to the kind of NYPD detective that is not stereotypical, and a continuing opportunity for the writers to create dramatic conflict with the new detective's partner, Mike Logan.

I decided that Cerreta would be a snappy dresser, because, in my head, I had given him parents who were in the haberdashery business. Initially, I had him in a three-piece suit until Joe Stern, my executive producer, rightly pointed out that Cerreta looked more like a banker than a police detective, so I had his wardrobe toned down. For the role, I had in mind one actor: Paul Sorvino. In fact, I filled in the details of Cerreta's life based on Sorvino himself. Sorvino, like his *Law & Order* alter ego, is an accomplished chef and a lover of opera who happens to sing tenor.

Cerreta was transferred into the 27th Precinct to head up the investigation of the shooting death of Max Greevey. He became Mike Logan's partner and, as it turns out, a very good foil for him. We built into the story the natural resentment that Logan felt in having Cerreta step into the shoes of his murdered partner. Yet, it quickly became clear that the almost fifty-year-old Cerreta was adept at handling the brash young Logan. As with Greevey, I gave Cerreta family—a wife and five children. Known for his compassion, Cerreta understood that his true badge of honor was his twenty years on the job without ever being called upon to shoot anybody.

Paul Sorvino decided to leave the show, principally to pursue a career in opera. In the episode "Prince of Darkness," Cerreta became the second of *Law & Order*'s detectives to be shot, although he wasn't killed. In the end, Phil Cerreta left the pages of *Law & Order* to transfer to a desk job in another precinct.

PAUL SORVINO AS DET. SGT. PHIL CERRETA (SEASONS TWO AND THREE)

LENNIE BRISCOE Detective

When Paul Sorvino left the series early in its third season, my choice of Jerry Orbach as his successor felt just right. In fact, Orbach had been a candidate for the show twice before—in 1988 and 1991—and had made a guest appearance as a defense attorney (in the episode "The Wages of Love"). When the opportunity arose, I didn't hesitate to offer him the character of Detective Lennie Briscoe.

When I first thought about Briscoe, I wanted a character from a mixed background, so I gave him a Jewish father and a Catholic mother. I envisioned Lennie Briscoe as a cop's cop, a cornerstone of the "blue wall," there to remind you that the old days "ain't going nowhere." Briscoe knows every nook and cranny of the city, including, importantly for him, where the best hot dog vendors are located. When he's off-duty, he can be found at OTB, shooting pool, or hanging out with other cops at a Mets game. And his mysterious lady friends? Although the writers have never "taken" him out on a date, don't be surprised if they're cops, too.

Briscoe uses his infamous wisecracks to cover the reality of too many dead bodies and too many disappointments. A recovering alcoholic, Briscoe drank his way through two marriages and the distancing of two daughters. Although he typically sloughs it off, Briscoe's feelings of guilt are transparent. His daughter Cathy, a drug addict, was shot by dealers—and it's clear that Briscoe blames himself for her murder because he was an absentee father. No matter how tough or cynical Briscoe may appear, the audience knows that underneath, he has a lot of internal conflict.

Briscoe is such a strong character, that were he to leave, I would truly miss him. Fortunately, he's not leaving the department any time in the near future. Although he has already lost two partners and is presently paired with his third, Briscoe's temperament remains constant. He has weathered the hotheaded Logan, the brooding, serious Reynaldo Curtis, and after taking a little time to adjust to Ed Green's demons, Briscoe's still doing what he does best: being Briscoe.

JERRY ORBACH AS DET. LENNIE BRISCOE (SEASONS THREE THROUGH PRESENT)

In season four, following NBC's dictate that I include two females in *Law & Order*'s cast, I wanted to create characters that truly reflected the role of women in the justice system. In reality, there are many women lawyers, so creating Assistant District Attorney Claire Kincaid was not as complex as crafting a high-ranking female officer for the traditionally male bastion of the police department. And with the loss of Assistant District Attorney Paul Robinette, I wanted to continue to give a voice to the city's large African American population. Thus, I created Lieutenant Anita Van Buren, who not only faces obstacles as a high-ranking woman in the force, but for whom racial bias is also an issue. To bring this character to life, I selected the extraordinary S. Epatha Merkerson.

Unlike her predecessor, Donald Cragen, I did not make Van Buren a captain. In giving her the lower rank of lieutenant, I was following my perception of how the system often withholds power from African Americans. In her backstory, Van Buren had been passed over for promotion to captain in favor of a lesser-qualified white woman. While she came to the squad room with an understandable chip on her shoulder, she also came as a woman with a lot of personal responsibility, as a wife and the mother of two young boys.

In the early stages of her development, Van Buren principally served in the capacity of the precinct's boss, with occasional victim interrogations and an initial confrontation with Logan, who was uncomfortable with a woman being in charge. Over time, her role expanded. In season five's "Competence," after shooting an unarmed teenager, Van Buren came under intense scrutiny by the Internal Affairs division. Ironically, it was Logan who rallied to her defense.

Van Buren sued the police department for discrimination, and although she lost, the force subtly penalized her for having initiated the lawsuit. Van Buren confronted her greatest crisis in season twelve's "Myth of Fingerprints," when she learned that the case by which she had been promoted to lieutenant had been a miscarriage of justice. This discovery has given Van Buren's quest for justice even greater focus, and she is seen more and more with her detectives, out on the street, searching for it.

S. EPATHA MERKERSON AS LT. ANITA VAN BUREN (SEASONS FOUR THROUGH PRESENT)

REYNALDO CURTIS Detective

When Detective Reynaldo (Rey) Curtis stepped into the script of "Bitter Fruit," he represented a new era for *Law & Order*'s police department. Curtis epitomized the transition of the show's detectives from "old world"—white, European, and traditional—to the "new"—Hispanic, multilingual, and hip. He was the modern cop, fluent in technology and popular culture. In addition, I gave the writers an opportunity to pair Briscoe with a character from Generation X, which allowed them to create edgier dialogue than had previously existed in the Briscoe-Logan pairing.

I wrote the character of Rey Curtis expressly for Benjamin Bratt. Tall, dark, and handsome, Curtis was a walking contradiction. He was fiercely opposed to the death penalty, yet not opposed to using lethal force to defend himself or others. He understood those whom society had discarded, but refused to let them use it as an excuse for criminal behavior.

I created more of a personal life for Curtis than had ever been shown on *Law & Order*. I was interested in having the fundamentally solid and straight-laced Curtis placed in situations that would test his values. Curtis was happily married, with three young daughters. But, he also had immense sexual appeal, which we played up by having him outfitted in tank tops. In fact, Curtis had transferred out of his former precinct because of propositions made to him by his female boss. Whether with his family or the force, Curtis took his vows very seriously. When the writers had him succumb to an extramarital affair, the audience was witness to his remorse.

Although the writers did not breach the line of actually "going home" with a character, we did take the unusual step of bringing his family into the "scene." In season seven, his wife, Deborah, was diagnosed with multiple sclerosis. Most unusual for *Law & Order,* Deborah made three on-screen visits—one of which was to the precinct. When Bratt eventually decided to leave *Law & Order* for cinematic horizons, we structured Curtis' exit around his family. On May 26, 1999, Curtis, trying to do the right thing, transferred out of the squad to take a desk job that afforded him more time to care for his ailing wife.

BENJAMIN BRATT AS DET. REYNALDO CURTIS (SEASONS SIX THROUGH NINE)

ED GREEN Detective

Detective Ed Green was the ideal replacement for his predecessor, the staid, prim Rey Curtis. My goal with cast changes is always to afford new creative opportunities for the writers. And with Fast Eddie (as his father nicknamed him), they've certainly been given more than a handful. Green arrived at *Law & Order*'s 27th Precinct armed with attitude— and with three prior complaints of excessive force in the field. It's taken quite some time for his new partner, Lennie Briscoe, to adjust to his complicated personality.

In deciding on who would fill the role of Green, I wanted an actor who could convey a streetwise attitude that was combined with a level of elegance. It only took one look at Jesse L. Martin to know that I'd found the perfect Ed Green. I envisioned Green as a guy who had grown up under somewhat unusual circumstances. I made him the son of a petrochemical engineer, who, from early childhood, had lived in many countries and become fluent in many languages. Green's nomadic youth left him with a sense of not quite knowing where he belongs. And as an African American, he has yet to resolve his comfortable life overseas with the racism he's experienced since returning to the states.

Green has underlying anger that's primarily fueled by his complicated relationship with his father. I created a situation in which Green, who became a cop against his father's wishes, has found himself truly dislocated. He has not spoken to his father in years and this personal conflict has contributed to his excessive use of force as well as to an unfortunate pattern of compulsive gambling.

Still, Ed Green's background has made him an asset to the department. He's comfortable with people from all walks of life, as demonstrated by his skill as an expert interrogator. He uses an easy, empathetic manner to gain a suspect's trust, and his years spent at poker tables make him an astute reader of "tells." If we can keep his emotions checked at the door and his hands off the cards, Ed Green may well have a long future in the 27th Precinct.

JESSE L. MARTIN AS DET. ED GREEN (SEASONS TEN THROUGH PRESENT)

BENJAMIN STONE Executive Assistant District Attorney

Central to my vision of *Law & Order* was the idea of the prosecutors as the heroes. Whereas television shows had typically focused on the defense, I was interested in exploring a new angle, one that I believed would afford a richer, more complete view of the justice system. However, I knew that there was a fine line between creating a character whose sole intention was to seek justice and one that seemed unrealistically perfect. With Ben Stone, my aim was to establish the character of the executive assistant district attorney as the moral conscience of the show, with an understanding that his strengths could also be his weaknesses. For this most pivotal role, I selected the brilliant actor, Michael Moriarty.

Stone's background included an alcoholic father, an ex-wife, and a daughter. Born and raised in New York City, he was of English-Irish ancestry. But his personality was most influenced by Catholicism. Ben Stone thought in terms of "right" and "just"—for him there was no gray area. Yet, Stone was in an arena where truth is often subjective and justice can be elusive. It was always my intent for *Law & Order* to portray the justice system as imperfect, where the prosecution would, as in reality, lose cases. Thus, Stone served as a foil for the justice system itself. Time and again, while the audience was witness to his anguish, it was also witness to him tripping over his own self-righteousness. Stone passionately wanted right to prevail, but with rare exception, would not sidestep the law to achieve his goal.

Although the pairings with his deputies Paul Robinette and Claire Kincaid gave the writers interesting fodder, arguably the most intense moments for Stone were those in which he was pitted against Defense Attorney Shambala Green (played by Lorraine Toussaint). Green challenged Stone's beliefs in and out of court, and together they exuded a level of strong personal attraction. Of all those surrounding Stone, Green was the one person who could cut through his didactic nature.

Michael was vocal in his decision to leave the show and it was widely reported in the press. I tried, to no avail, to convince him to stay. In his final episode, "Old Friends," his principles contributed to his downfall, and *Law & Order* lost its first executive ADA.

MICHAEL MORIARTY AS EXECUTIVE ADA BEN STONE (PILOT EPISODE AND SEASONS ONE THROUGH FOUR)

PAUL ROBINETTE Assistant District Attorney

The character of Paul Robinette was critical to my original vision of *Law & Order.* I wanted all the show's characters to represent varying perspectives and to be truly connected to the culture and the realities of New York City—which has a significant African American community. Furthermore, in developing the prosecutorial side of the show—which I have often referred to as "the moral mystery"—I wanted to include a character whose background spoke to the disenfranchised. And so I created Assistant District Attorney Paul Robinette, played by the gifted Richard Brooks.

The backstory for Robinette included a disadvantaged childhood in Harlem. Robinette was a guy who had pulled himself up by his bootstraps, earning scholarships through college and law school. He had eschewed offers from prestigious Wall Street law firms to take a spot with the district attorney's office, where he felt that he could make a difference. When I paired him with Ben Stone, I wanted Robinette to serve as a foil to Stone's idealism. Where Stone saw things as they should be, Robinette saw things as they were. Race, for Robinette, was not an excuse, but a reality—something not to be exploited, yet not to be ignored.

Robinette never tried a single case during his tenure; rather, he handled the nuances of the cases and acted as a bridge between the cops and his office. Of course, the realities of the system were always there and the cases were often personal tests. As a black man in the justice system, Robinette occasionally experienced conflict. In the episode "Out of the Halflight," when Stone asks Robinette to decide if he's a black man who is a lawyer or a lawyer who happens to be black, he has no answer.

At the end of season three, upon NBC's insistence, I had to replace Brooks with another minority: a female. Although his tenure as an ADA concluded on May 19, 1993, Robinette returned in season six for a guest appearance in the episode "Custody"—this time as a civil rights defense attorney. The change in Robinette went far beyond the loss of his trademark "flattop" hairdo. Apart from finally getting to argue a case and stumping the prosecution, he had an answer to his earlier doubts, coming back to his roots as a black man, who happens to be a lawyer.

RICHARD BROOKS AS ADA PAUL ROBINETTE (THE PILOT EPISODE AND SEASONS ONE THROUGH THREE)

Were it not for a scheduling problem, District Attorney Adam Schiff might never have had a line in a *Law & Order* script (or a bite of his trademark tuna fish sandwich). In the show's 1988 pilot, actor Roy Thinnes played the role of District Attorney Alfred Wentworth. However, by the time *Law & Order* was picked up in 1990, Roy was committed elsewhere, and thus DA Wentworth was replaced by DA Adam Schiff. For the role, I selected the seamless actor, Steven Hill.

In the pilot, our characters had consisted of four Irishmen, one African American, and one WASP (Wentworth). New York City has a large Jewish population, and I realized that with Schiff, a Jew, we could add more reality and texture to the show. In keeping with his roots, I gave Schiff a vision of the justice system that bordered on Talmudic—making him essential to *Law & Order*'s exploration of the ethical and moral underpinnings of the law. Schiff's office was a respite for his prosecutors from the front lines of the legal wars, where they could discuss cases whose ramifications often went beyond the innocence or guilt of a particular defendant.

The character of Adam Schiff was created to be very politically liberal. In the 1960s, he had been a defense attorney for anti-war protesters. And he was an old-school believer that the system should rehabilitate, rather than simply punish offenders. Yet his years on the job took their toll—from watching his old friends from politics fall by the legal wayside, to his very personal decision to remove the life-support system from his wife, who had suffered a stroke. As Schiff's character evolved, he became increasingly pragmatic and the phrase "cut a deal" became his mantra.

At the end of season ten, Hill opted out of the show. On May 24, 2000, in the appropriately titled episode "Vaya Con Dios" (Go with God), the last of *Law & Order*'s original characters said good-bye to his job as district attorney, moved to Vienna, and became an advocate for victims of the Holocaust.

STEVEN HILL AS DA ADAM SCHIFF (SEASONS ONE THROUGH TEN)

CLAIRE KINCAID Assistant District Attorney

The introduction of Claire Kincaid clearly brought a new dimension to the show. In hindsight, the network's insistence that I add female characters to the cast was fortuitous, not only because it afforded new opportunities for the writers, but also because it brought a broader sensibility to *Law & Order*. Apart from the decision to bring in a female lieutenant, Anita Van Buren, I decided that the district attorney's office should have a character that could represent a solidly new perspective. For the role of Claire Kincaid, Ben Stone's new deputy ADA, I selected the talented young actress, Jill Hennessy.

With Kincaid, the district attorney's office gained a staunch feminist—and the most politically left-wing character ever to appear on *Law & Order*. Although Kincaid was the product of a privileged, Harvard Law School background, she had compassion and sympathy for those less fortunate. While her idealism and sensitivity would have seemed more suited to a job as a public defender, the fact that she chose prosecution reflected her need to bring balance to that side of the law. It wasn't that Kincaid didn't believe in punishment for criminal acts. Rather, unlike most prosecutors, she cared about the underlying reasons for the commission of the acts themselves.

The development of Kincaid's character took some time. She came into the job to find that her work was primarily adjunctive to Ben Stone's. Her only prior professional experience had been as a law clerk; thus, Kincaid was virtually Stone's student throughout her initial season. It wasn't until the following season, when Jack McCoy arrived to take over as the executive assistant district attorney, that the writers gave her real dimension and allowed her to find her voice. In seasons five and six, Kincaid grew more independent and developed into the moral conscience of her office. As for the hints of an affair with McCoy, with whom she became an excellent sparring partner—did she or didn't she? I will only say that her death from injuries suffered in a car crash in the episode "Aftershock" left Jack McCoy at a loss that was clearly more than professional.

JILL HENNESSY AS ADA CLAIRE KINCAID (SEASONS FOUR THROUGH SIX)

JACK MCCOY Executive Assistant District Attorney

When NBC executives expressed concern about how to replace Michael Moriarty's Ben Stone, I had two words for them: Sam Waterston. As soon as I knew that Michael was leaving the show, I had a gut instinct that Sam would be an excellent replacement. In the continuing tradition of having characters represent varying perspectives, I determined that the new executive assistant district attorney would have a personality in direct contrast to his predecessor. As opposed to the moral center that drove Stone, the impetus for our new character, Jack McCoy, would be his need to win.

McCoy's arrival in the episode "Second Opinion" brought a whole new energy to his office. McCoy drinks Scotch, rides to work on a motorcycle, and, after work, can't wait to get back into his dungarees—all of which would have been unimaginable to Ben Stone. Divorced, with one daughter, Jack has made the most of his bachelor life. He's a bit of a fox and he moves quickly, especially when charming women. Hints of his affairs have been threaded throughout the scripts, and his initial meeting with Claire Kincaid set up a dynamic that would continue throughout her tenure. Yet, since Kincaid, McCoy has had three female deputies—Jamie Ross, Abbie Carmichael, and Serena Southerlyn—all of whom have been immune to his romantic charm.

Jack McCoy is the child of a working-class family. His father, a sometimes brutal Chicago cop, reveled in Jack's successes and became violent at his failures. Like Stone, McCoy received a Catholic education. But, while Stone became the true believer, McCoy is the consummate doubter. While Stone was in constant search for the truth, McCoy is driven by sheer intellectual combativeness. While Stone wanted the right result, McCoy just wants to win.

McCoy attended law school at NYU, graduating first in his class. He had numerous offers to join top-flight New York law firms where a high salary would have wiped out his school financial loans. Instead, he thought he'd get a little seasoning for "a few years" in the hard-knocks school of the Manhattan DA's office. Those few years have turned into almost twenty. It seems that Jack loves his job, almost as much as he loves to win.

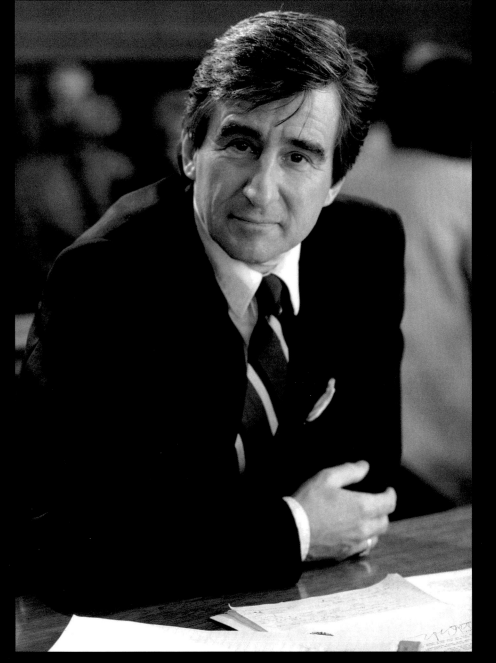

SAM WATERSTON AS EXECUTIVE ADA JACK MCCOY (SEASONS FIVE THROUGH PRESENT)

JAMIE ROSS Assistant District Attorney

With Claire Kincaid having paved the way, I was interested in casting another female as the next deputy ADA. My idea was to have this character be more mature and, thus, more seasoned than the young, idealistic Kincaid. In fact, the writers themselves were more seasoned in developing this part for a woman, having learned a lot while evolving Kincaid's character. Our new ADA, Jamie Ross, was not arriving as a novice, who would begin her tenure as a student to Jack McCoy. Instead, the intent was to fill the vacancy with a woman for whom gender was not a driving force, and who would not be intimidated by her male counterpart. In Carey Lowell, I found the perfect Jamie Ross.

The basic structure of Ross' character was fashioned, in part, from Carey's background. Carey, for example, comes from a large family, so a similar one was written into Ross' backstory. Moreover, when Carey was cast, she was divorced and a single mother; thus, we gave Ross an ex-husband and a young daughter. In her first episode, "Causa Mortis," it was revealed that Ross had been a defense attorney in her ex-husband's firm. But more important was the dynamic between Ross and McCoy. Ross held her ground and aggressively expressed her opinions, even in the face of McCoy's initial resentment of her as Kincaid's replacement. During her tenure, Ross confronted sexual harassment, personal betrayal, and underlying problems with her ex-husband—and in every situation remained tough and empathetic.

When, at the end of season eight, Carey wanted to leave the show to spend more time with her daughter, we built that into the script. Jamie Ross left the DA's office to remarry, in part, to improve her position in a custody battle with her ex-husband. In her final episode as a cast member, "Monster," a little twist was added. In keeping with her independent spirit, we had Ross leave McCoy dangling about her testimony concerning him at a disciplinary hearing. Although Jamie Ross was to reappear in two later episodes, "Justice" and "School Daze," her return was not to the DA's office. Instead, she appeared in court as a defense attorney and a formidable opponent to Jack McCoy.

CAREY LOWELL AS ADA JAMIE ROSS (SEASONS SEVEN AND EIGHT)

ABBIE CARMICHAEL Assistant District Attorney

After Carey Lowell's departure from *Law & Order*, I took a chance on hiring Angie Harmon, a young, inexperienced actress to fill the opening in the DA's office. With her striking presence, raspy voice, and Texas accent, I saw an opportunity to build a strong, tough-talking, combative character that would play well against Jack McCoy.

Of all of the ADAs to appear on *Law & Order,* Abbie Carmichael was clearly the most outspoken. She first arrived in the DA's office in the episode "Cherished," and got down to business before McCoy knew what hit him. Although his last ADA, Jamie Ross, was hardly a pushover, Carmichael was a virtual brick wall. In this pairing, obviously, I wanted to promote strong conflict. But, I also wanted to underline the differences in prosecutors who may ultimately have the same goal, yet approach it with very dissimilar mind-sets. Carmichael, unlike McCoy, was completely doctrinaire. She viewed her job as a mission, skirting the line between prosecution and persecution. While McCoy's motto has always been "hang 'em high," Carmichael's motto was "hang 'em higher."

When I drew this character, I wanted to give psychological justification for her motivation to win at all costs. I worked into her backstory the fact that as a freshman in college, she had been date-raped by a third-year law student, who, through a loophole in the law, avoided punishment. Thus, Carmichael always saw herself as a victim in search of justice. Her single-minded dedication to this personal crusade led to an unprecedented ninety-five percent conviction rate at her prior job in the Special Narcotics Division. Eventually, the writers allowed occasional cracks in her demeanor, making her more sympathetic. But, essentially, Carmichael always remained wedded to her judicial principles.

At the end of season eleven, when Angie was leaving the show, we decided to give Carmichael a job where she could truly satisfy her need for vengeance. On May 23, 2001, Abbie Carmichael said good-bye to Jack McCoy and walked into her new job in the U.S. Attorney's Office as a prosecutor for the Federal Major Crimes Task Force.

ANGIE HARMON AS ADA ABBIE CARMICHAEL (SEASONS NINE THROUGH ELEVEN)

NORA LEWIN District Attorney

With Steven Hill leaving the show, there were big shoes to be filled in selecting a new district attorney. Hill's Adam Schiff had become a legend during his long *Law & Order* tenure, and when word of his departure leaked out, there was a very angry reaction from the show's fans. I felt an obligation to them to find a replacement that would measure up to their expectations, and so I dedicated a lot of time and energy to selecting an actor whom I felt the audience would embrace.

First, I was clear that hiring a male actor would only heighten the possibility of comparisons, so I was set on hiring a female. I then went through a list of potential candidates. When Dianne Wiest came to mind, I felt that she was the perfect choice. Not only was Wiest's presence so significantly different from what the fans were used to in the district attorney, here was an opportunity to hire an Academy Award–winning movie actress. I tried to give Wiest as much leeway as possible to develop her character, including selecting her name: Nora Lewin.

When Nora Lewin finally took over the reigns as the interim DA (in the episode "Endurance"), she was understandably nervous to be following the legendary Adam Schiff. Unlike her predecessor, Lewin's experience had not been on the battlegrounds of the courtroom, but in the classrooms of Brooklyn Law School, where her area of expertise had been legal ethics. Thus, she always felt an underlying accusation from her staff that she had an "ivory tower" detachment from the sometimes dirty world of plea-bargaining and prosecutorial high jinks. Although, like Schiff, Lewin was politically liberal, she did not have his political instinct for compromise, holding firmly to her idealistic beliefs. As her tenure wore on, however, Lewin became more of a realist.

Over time Lewin came to understand that her duty to uphold the law was more important than her personal political bent. Yet she was never fully comfortable in her prosecutorial skin. After her two-year interim term, Nora Lewin opted not to run for election. On May 22, 2002, viewers said good-bye to *Law & Order's* first female district attorney.

DIANNE WIEST AS DA NORA LEWIN (SEASONS ELEVEN AND TWELVE)

SERENA SOUTHERLYN Assistant District Attorney

Although every cast change on *Law & Order* is given a lot of thought, season twelve's vacancy in the district attorney's office brought a special challenge. Jack McCoy had been the executive ADA for seven seasons and in that time, had had three female deputies, each with very different and distinctive personalities. I knew that I was going to give McCoy another female ADA, but it was necessary to devise a character that could maintain a level of dramatic conflict without seeming reiterative. I decided that the best solution was a character that, initially, would be a mixture of predecessors Kincaid and Ross, yet whose own perspective and prejudices would evolve over time. For this new character, Serena Southerlyn, I selected Elisabeth Röhm.

In her backstory, I gave Southerlyn an East Coast sophistication. She's the daughter of a Wall Street lawyer and has had an Ivy League education. Having lived a relatively sheltered life, Southerlyn was curious to explore other dimensions. Thus, rather than take a job in the private sector, she chose to work in public service. Fresh out of law school, her first job was in civil investigations. Finding the work unsatisfying, Southerlyn transferred into the district attorney's office, when McCoy offered her the job as his deputy. She first appears in the episode "Who Let the Dogs Out?"

Like Kincaid, Southerlyn is young, unmarried, and from a privileged background. Also like Kincaid, Southerlyn comes to the job with an eagerness to learn and her early relationship with her boss is tutorial. But, unlike Kincaid, Southerlyn does not come with her predecessor's staunch feminist agenda. Like Ross, she is more interested in the business of the law. While Kincaid became more self-assured as time went on, Southerlyn has more quickly displayed the kind of strength seen in Ross. Although McCoy is still her mentor, Southerlyn has been straining at the leash.

That Southerlyn traded in her pearl necklace look for a more urban wardrobe is emblematic of her growing understanding of the real world. Her wide-eyed naïveté has, thus far, been transformed by the eye-opening realities of an imperfect justice system. Ultimately, like Kincaid and Ross, Serena Southerlyn cares about doing the right thing.

ELISABETH RÖHM AS ADA SERENA SOUTHERLYN (SEASONS TWELVE THROUGH PRESENT)

The creation of Arthur Branch, *Law & Order*'s current district attorney, was a risky decision. When I first proposed creating a conservative Republican DA for New York County, there was widespread belief at *Law & Order* that it would not be a realistic choice. This job had historically been the domain of liberal Democrats, and given the high percentage of Democratic voters in the county, it did not appear likely to change. But the fact of the matter was that many of our beliefs and assurances disappeared with the Twin Towers on 9/11. In the tradition of *Law & Order*, I wanted this most definitive moment to be reflected in our vision.

Fred Thompson was an easy choice for the part. Prior to his election as a United States senator from Tennessee, Thompson had had a flourishing acting career. There was only one problem: Arthur Branch was needed immediately in our district attorney's office in New York, but Fred Thompson was still a sitting senator in Washington, D.C. Although he was giving up his seat at the end of 2002, our shooting schedule began a few months earlier. Somehow things worked out and Thompson did not have to miss a vote (or a line).

Apart from his conservative political views, I had to justify the fact of a Manhattan district attorney with a strong southern drawl. Thus, I figured out a reasonable backstory for Branch. Although raised in Georgia, Arthur Branch graduated from Yale Law School. Soon thereafter, he married a native New Yorker, Lillian, and joined the litigation department of a Manhattan law firm. In record time, he earned a partnership and, through the years, made many powerful contacts. Tired of defending Fortune 500 clients, he simply used these contacts to help him make a bid for office. Following 9/11, New Yorkers were comforted by Branch's homespun yarns and his no-nonsense, direct approach to fixing problems, and elected him to office. So, why after thirty-five years in New York has Branch not lost his deep Southern accent? The answer is that he's smart, and in his years as a litigator he's learned to use the accent to charm juries—the accent has simply become part of his style.

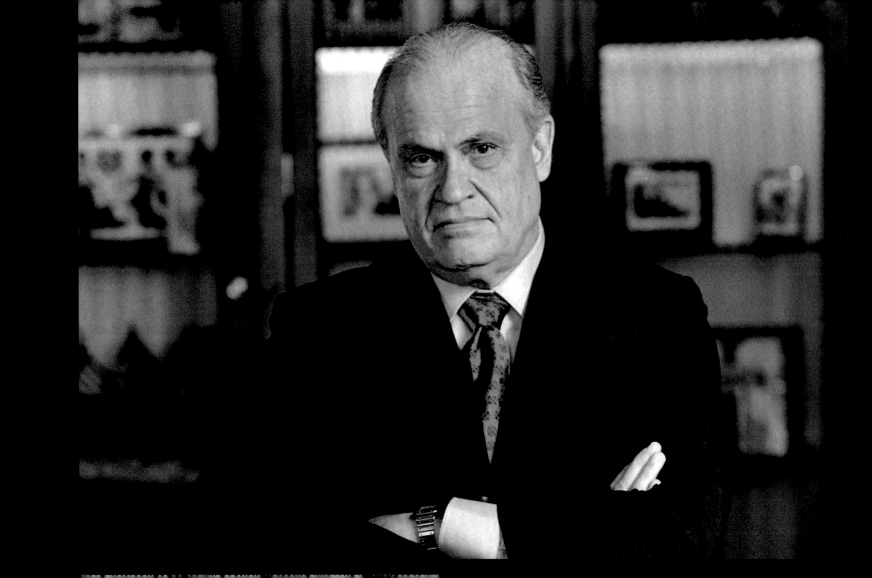

POSTMORTEM

EPISODE 85: "SANCTUARY," ORIGINAL NBC AIRDATE: APRIL 13, 1994 (PAGE 61)
This was the first crime scene I'd shot, as well as the first time that I'd ever set foot at *Law & Order*. Shooting on the Upper West Side of Manhattan, the scene involved a large number of people and a lot of action. With so much activity, I couldn't visually isolate the core of the scene. I shot a lot of film, but felt that nothing was working to capture the overall picture. In the end, I went with my instinct that, in this case, rather than show the details of what happened, the photographs needed only to say that *something* had happened. Although I have combed through the contact sheets for this crime scene innumerable times, I always return to this shot—and the one on page 109—which I believe encapsulate the true feel of this scene.

EPISODE 113: "REBELS," ORIGINAL NBC AIRDATE: SEPTEMBER 27, 1995 (PAGE 63)
This crime scene was filmed outside of the well-known bar Hogs & Heifers on Little West 12th Street in the city's meatpacking district. The photograph is truly an illusion, considering the amount of activity that surrounded it. There were at least thirty motorcycle bikers who'd been hired as extras and an equal number of motorcycles revved up to a deafening roar. Because the bikers were not actors, and thus not what is termed "set-wise," the location was chaotic. Since it took so much time to get things under control, the director opted to shoot without a rehearsal, and my only opportunity to photograph the crime scene was during the takes. In order to avoid hearing the shutter click in the scene, I was forced to place the camera in a soundproofing device known as a "blimp."

EPISODE 105: "ACT OF GOD," ORIGINAL NBC AIRDATE: MARCH 22, 1995 (PAGES 66 & 67)
Numerous elements went into this scene that was shot in a deserted area of central Harlem, including assorted vehicles and an extraordinary number of extras. The location department was fortunate to find a building that was in the process of being destroyed to make way for new housing, and the city generously agreed to allow *Law & Order* to shoot there. In order to create the illusion of a large explosion, a lot of work went into constructing the scene, including the placement of massive pieces of wood and the piling up of huge rocks. With the addition of the special effects' smoke, filming became treacherous as people tried not to trip over debris. Extreme care was taken to ensure everyone's safety, and only a limited number of people were allowed into the fray. As a result, I had to be very aggressive (and a little sneaky) to get the shots.

EPISODE 145: "MENACE," ORIGINAL NBC AIRDATE: FEBRUARY 5, 1997 (PAGE 64)
It was an ice-cold night when this crime scene was shot, under the Williamsburg Bridge in lower Manhattan. Because the dead body was barely clothed, between takes wardrobe would immediately step in to cover her with a blanket—leaving me, in the end, with perhaps three seconds to capture the shot. I only managed to get a meager two frames. Considering what the dead body had to go through, I was very lucky.

EPISODE 222: "BLACK, WHITE AND BLUE," ORIGINAL NBC AIRDATE: MARCH 22, 2000 (PAGE 65)
Because of a scheduling change, I arrived at the location on the Upper West Side after the crime scene had concluded. Fortunately, the dead body was still around, eating lunch in the craft service truck. With help from the hair and makeup departments and the set scenic, the dead body agreed to interrupt his lunch to enable us to recreate the scene. The actor was a great sport. After having spent all that time lying on the cold, dirty ground, he was happily willing to do it all over again.

EPISODE 105: "ACT OF GOD," ORIGINAL NBC AIRDATE: MARCH 22, 1995 (PAGE 68)
The "victim" of the explosion was a real trouper. Not only did this little boy have to tolerate several applications of the "blood" that was created to stream down his face, but he was also very tightly wrapped in a blanket that was tied to a stretcher. He then had to brave several takes in which he was lifted on the stretcher and carried up and down a large mound of debris. By the time I flashed this shot, the actor was so shell-shocked, it aided the illusion.

EPISODE 227: "HIGH & LOW," ORIGINAL NBC AIRDATE: MAY 17, 2000 (PAGE 69)
This is the only image in the book that was not shot in New York City. We were working in Atlantic Beach, Long Island. The shot was also not part of an actual scene in the episode. I had already shot the episode's crime scene (page 70) and I was on location for a publicity shoot. As I was leaving, I noticed this actress dressed for an upcoming scene patiently sitting on a boardwalk step. I was stunned by how real the bruises appeared. I said hello, she looked up at me, and I shot.

 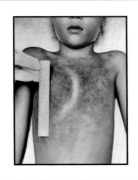

EPISODE 227: "HIGH & LOW," ORIGINAL NBC AIRDATE: MAY 17, 2000 (PAGE 70)
I owe this shot, which was taken in an Upper West Side building, to the episode's director, Richie Dobbs. As a director, Richie has been my virtual "partner-in-crime-scenes," which is to say that he has a very sensitive touch for this kind of work. The dead body was not initially scripted to be found in the bathtub. But, Richie felt that the shot would be more evocative if the victim were to be placed as she appears in this photograph. His instinct was correct and this is one of my favorite images.

EPISODE 168: "UNDER THE INFLUENCE," ORIGINAL NBC AIRDATE: JANUARY 7,1998 (PAGE 71)
Taken in the "morgue" at *Law & Order*'s stages, this shot required extra delicacy since our actor was only nine years old. He was patient throughout the makeup session, during which wounds were created to show that he'd been run over by a car. And because the morgue table is high, I had to stand on top of it to shoot down. The table is also very narrow, leaving little room for the "victim" and me. This can be scary for anyone, but especially for a child lying there who must relax in order to play dead. This little boy admirably handled a difficult situation.

EPISODE 165: "SHADOW," ORIGINAL NBC AIRDATE: NOVEMBER 26,1997 (PAGE 72)
The location was a street-level office in a building on Tenth Avenue in the Chelsea district of Manhattan. The space was so tight that there was barely enough room for a minimal camera crew and the actors. Everyone else was banished to the street. Each time I tried to sneak in, I was rebuffed, and it was beginning to look hopeless for stills. Ultimately, Jerry and Ben took matters into their own hands and swept me inside. Nobody argues with the cast (usually), and so I got the shot.

EPISODE 229: "VAYA CON DIOS," ORIGINAL NBC AIRDATE: MAY 24, 2000 (PAGE 73)
What was memorable about this crime scene filmed in an Upper West Side building was the sheer joy the actor took in playing dead. Eventually we learned that his first acting job, at the age of six, had been as a dead body. The job had been in a theatrical production and, according to his story, was the moment he became hooked on acting. Apparently, this *Law & Order* episode was the first time in more than fifty years that he got to play dead, and he couldn't have been more delighted.

 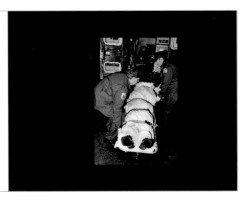

EPISODE 226: "NARCOSIS," ORIGINAL NBC AIRDATE: MAY 10, 2000 (PAGE 74)
This scene was shot inside an empty Hudson River enclosed pier, where the crew had dressed two cargo containers: one containing "enslaved immigrants" and the second representing the conditions in which the women had been held. This shoot was difficult because the actors seemed to find either me or the situation amusing. Invariably, one or another of the women would start laughing— which became contagious. Although I shot numerous frames, this was the only one in which I caught them all looking suitably serious

EPISODE 277: "PATRIOT," ORIGINAL NBC AIRDATE: MAY 22, 2002 (PAGE 75)
The crime scene from "Patriot" is noteworthy because it was created from scratch at *Law & Order*'s stages. This scene truly exemplifies the brilliance of the art department in designing illusions. All I had to do was show up and shoot. (Note: This was Dianne Wiest's final episode.)

EPISODE 223: "MEGA," ORIGINAL NBC AIRDATE: APRIL 5, 2000 (PAGE 76)
This crime scene was shot at a former heliport, adjacent to the East River. I had difficulty capturing this image. First, there were no dead bodies shown in the scene—just body bags with paper stuffed inside—so I had to wander around for quite some time to find something of visual interest. And because it was a morning with very bright sunlight bouncing off the water, I could only shoot from one direction without the light casting heavy shadows or causing flare. Ultimately, I found a position and waited for something to happen.

EPISODE 111: "PRIDE," ORIGINAL NBC AIRDATE: MAY 24, 1995 (PAGE 77)
Shot in the West Village, this crime scene was very emotional because it was to be the last one for Chris Noth, who was leaving the show. Although I also photographed the dead body when he was lying on the street, I preferred this image not only because it struck me as eerie, but because in some inexplicable way, it also captured the feeling of the entire night. Should anyone be curious, there was indeed an actual live person under the sheet.

EPISODE 203: "ADMISSIONS," ORIGINAL NBC AIRDATE: MAY 19, 1999 (PAGES 78 & 79)
The dead body of a college student was filmed where she was to be found in the script—on a college campus. Although the campus was supposed to be an unidentified one in Manhattan, in fact, we shot the scene in Brooklyn. The body did very well lying in the dirt among the bushes. But she was truly amazing in the morgue photograph that showed the wounds to her torso. The process of creating the wounds took hours and required exceptional patience from the actress. It was also a testament to the artistry of the then make-up supervisor, Patricia Regan. The makeup application first had to be done for the crime scene and then replicated for the morgue shot, requiring extraordinary precision. With Patricia's brilliant work, the morgue photograph was the equivalent of a gift handed to me.

EPISODE 158: "THRILL," ORIGINAL NBC AIRDATE: SEPTEMBER 24, 1997 (PAGE 80)
This shoot took place in Tribeca on a side street across from City Hall. It was the first episode of season eight and with the cast and crew just back from hiatus, there was high energy on the set. While I waited to photograph the scene, it was interesting to stand back and watch the intensity with which the crew worked. In doing their jobs, people were continuously and ever so casually stepping over the dead body. I'm sure that the dead body was not terribly comfortable, but, hey, anything for showbiz.

EPISODE 109: "PURPLE HEART," ORIGINAL NBC AIRDATE: MAY 3, 1995 (PAGE 81)
Located on the lower West Side in Manhattan's Chelsea district, this crime scene was easy to shoot. I was given enough time in which to do the work, as well as an extremely cooperative dead body. In fact, what is most memorable about this crime scene is that the actor played dead so well that it was virtually impossible to get a bad shot of him.

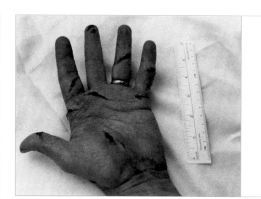 

EPISODE 112: "BITTER FRUIT," ORIGINAL NBC AIRDATE: SEPTEMBER 20, 1995 (PAGE 82)
By the time I arrived, the crew and the equipment trucks had already left the location, a Korean deli on the Lower East Side of Manhattan. I was with the art director and a Traffic Control Division officer who was there to prevent potential customers from entering the store. While shooting, I was suddenly interrupted by ear-piercing screams. Apparently, at some point, the police officer had moved inside and two customers stumbled into what they thought was a real crime scene. It momentarily threw me off, but the actor never even flinched. (Note: This was Ben Bratt's first episode.)

EPISODE 181: "MONSTER," ORIGINAL NBC AIRDATE: MAY 20, 1998 (PAGE 83)
Our young actress did a fine job of playing dead in this scene, which was filmed in the basement of an East Harlem housing project. But the real star of this crime scene was a trained rat named Rizzo. The scene opened with Rizzo scurrying across a low wall. For each of about five takes, the rat wrangler would whisper in his ear. Then, as "action" was called, Rizzo would run exactly to his mark. A good portion of my time that day was spent filling the crew's requests to be photographed with the little star. (Note: This was Carey Lowell's last episode as a cast member.)

EPISODE 106: "PRIVILEGED," ORIGINAL NBC AIRDATE: APRIL 5, 1995 (PAGES 84 & 85)
Located in a townhouse near Central Park West, this crime scene required almost a full day to photograph. The scene was changed various times, from the placement of the bodies to the blood that the make-up artists and scenics continuously recreated. I shot the dead body's hand on top of a sheet in the makeup truck, where Make-up Artist Carla White was working magic. During this shoot, I understood for the first time the extraordinary artistry of the makeup department. Because the hand was to be featured in an evidence shot, it required exactitude, and Carla spent hours referring to her forensics books and creating the wounds. "Privileged" was the one *Law & Order* episode that was not allowed release for replay on NBC because the network felt that it was too gory—it was only allowed to re-air in syndication. (The only other episode that presently will never re-air is "Sunday in the Park with Jorge," but not because of excessive blood. Rather, the episode so enraged the Puerto Rican community, that the decision not to re-release it is political.)

EPISODE 282: "THE RING," ORIGINAL NBC AIRDATE: NOVEMBER 6, 2002 (PAGE 86)
I took this evidence shot outside of the *Law & Order* stages at Chelsea Piers. The art director and the set scenic worked really hard to dress the arm in the photograph, adding varying amounts of ash and sand as well as placing litter in the appropriate places. It took a long time to get it right, but it turned out to be the best fake arm ever created by the show. The photograph is notable because it represented the first *Law & Order* episode that was based on 9/11.

EPISODE 204: "REFUGE" (PART ONE), ORIGINAL NBC AIRDATE: MAY 26, 1999 (PAGE 87)
This photograph was taken in *Law & Order*'s morgue. The only unusual aspect of the shoot was that I was not required, as I generally have been, to shoot from on top of the morgue table. Other than that, what can I say about a foot? I suppose it's worth mentioning that the actor remained very steady and, in consequence, the foot remained in position throughout the shoot. As for the Russian "tattoos," I no longer recall the translation for the writing.

EPISODE 219: "ENTITLED" (PART TWO), ORIGINAL NBC AIRDATE: FEBRUARY 18, 2000 (PAGE 88)
Filmed on an open pier overlooking the Hudson River, this crime scene was technically complex. The grips rigged a car to be hoisted up and then lowered onto the pier, as if it had been recovered from the river. When the car was lowered onto the pier, the body was then placed inside, creating the illusion that she had been submersed inside the car. This part of the scene was very tough on the actress, because it was an extremely cold day and she had to be constantly soaked in water.

EPISODE 205: "REFUGE" (PART TWO), ORIGINAL NBC AIRDATE: MAY 26, 1999 (PAGE 89)
This night shoot took place in a building in the East Village near Avenue A. Because there were two dead bodies in the scene, a variety of takes were necessary and filming went much slower than anticipated. When I heard that the final take, or "martini shot," was concluding, I raced up the stairs and ran smack into one of the two dead bodies—who, to my horror, was racing down. Informing her that I needed to document the crime scene, she was adamant about leaving to catch a bus. I replied that if she didn't get back upstairs, there'd be a real crime scene, on the spot. (Note: This crime scene was the final one for Ben Bratt.)

EPISODE 94: "COMPETENCE," ORIGINAL NBC AIRDATE: NOVEMBER 2, 1994 (PAGES 90 & 91)
Shot on Columbus Avenue on the West Side of Manhattan, this was a pivotal crime scene; in the episode, S. Epatha Merkerson's character, Anita Van Buren, has shot a teenager. It was also the only episode in which the viewers saw Van Buren's children—two young boys pictured here, on the right. This was one of two nighttime crime scenes for which I did not use a strobe (the other crime scene was for episode 113: "Rebels"). However, in this case, it was purposeful. I wanted the shadowy atmospheric look that a strobe would have flattened. Epatha, as always, was extremely generous in making certain that I got what I needed.

EPISODE 122: "CORPUS DELICTI," ORIGINAL NBC AIRDATE: JANUARY 17, 1996 (PAGE 92)
A riding academy in Riverdale, the Bronx, hosted this crime scene. The horse, whose character's name was Mr. Wickers, was slightly high-strung and it was a delicate shoot. His trainer had to calm him down a few times, and she remained hidden in the stall throughout. Remarkably, Mr. Wickers ended up playing dead better than many human actors in *Law & Order*'s crime scenes. This photograph is one of two in the book that required the use of the sound blimp.

EPISODE 241: "TEENAGE WASTELAND," ORIGINAL NBC AIRDATE: FEBRUARY 7, 2001 (PAGE 93)
Filmed on the Lower East Side in Alphabet City, this crime scene inexplicably attracted numerous bystanders who were convinced that the dead body was real. I suspect that somebody in the neighborhood had started a rumor that clearly got out of control. The fact is that the body was lying on a staircase at basement level, so the public could not actually see him. All they saw were police cars and the attendant "officers" milling around. It was an interesting moment when our body emerged alive, to the delight of the neighborhood.

EPISODE 134: "AFTERSHOCK," ORIGINAL NBC AIRDATE: MAY 22, 1996 (PAGE 94)
This night crime scene, shot in the West Village, concluded Jill Hennessy's last episode as a cast member. Thus, the shoot felt very intimate and emotional. When filming wrapped, we presented Jill with one of the car's hubcaps, signed by everyone—giving her a needed laugh. Although her character was eventually killed off, Jill, when in New York, still visits with *Law & Order*'s cast and crew.

EPISODE 157: "TERMINAL," ORIGINAL NBC AIRDATE: MAY 21, 1997 (PAGE 95)
This crime scene was shot at the dock of Chelsea Pier 61 on the Hudson River. I was shooting towards one of the two dead bodies, until I noticed that an actor playing the crime scene photographer was in my shot. Because I am, in essence, assuming the role of the crime scene photographer, it would have seemed odd for him to appear in my photographs. And so when he wouldn't move, I was forced to shoot from other angles. (Note: This was one of the rare times that *Law & Order* has used gunfire in a scene.)

EPISODE 121: "REMAND," ORIGINAL NBC AIRDATE: JANUARY 10, 1996 (PAGES 96 & 97)
Filmed in an open lot off the West Side Highway, this crime scene was visually complicated. It was a fairly large production, which included building a burnt-out shack, creating a very large sign, and adding numerous elements of set dressing. The makeup was also challenging, since the dead body needed to look "cooked" from a fire. When there's a lot going on, as there was during this shoot, it often becomes difficult to get the shot. I waited for a few hours until there was enough calm to move in for the "kill." It was a very cold night and not the most pleasant experience.

EPISODE 292: "B*TCH," ORIGINAL NBC AIRDATE: FEBRUARY 26, 2003 (PAGE 98)
The most notable aspect of this crime scene, filmed in the East Seventies, was that I shot it with a fractured wrist. My assistant held the camera and helped me to focus. The situation would have been easier if the dead body had been more cooperative. At first, he didn't take direction well and I had to keep yelling, "Play dead!" Finally, he relaxed, closed his eyes, and I got the shot.

EPISODE 265: "UNDERCOVERED," ORIGINAL NBC AIRDATE: JANUARY 16, 2002 (PAGE 99, TOP)
This crime scene was photographed on the Upper West Side off Riverside Drive. It was the first day that I returned to *Law & Order* after 9/11. Shooting the crime scene felt uncomfortable and I was as tentative as I had been when I'd first begun this project.

EPISODE 255: "ARMED FORCES," ORIGINAL NBC AIRDATE: OCTOBER 3, 2001 (PAGE 99, BOTTOM)
Shot on a warm July night, the crime scene took place on a small side street in Greenwich Village. Here's where I would have really liked to have had a wide shot, because the street had so much texture. But the crew and equipment in the area precluded that possibility, and I had to shoot more tightly.

EPISODE 118: "HUMILIATION," ORIGINAL NBC AIRDATE: NOVEMBER 22, 1995 (PAGE 100)
Filming took place in an alleyway in the West Forties, in the city's theater district. For the still images, I spent most of my time crouching down to shoot the dead body full-length, with her spiked heels in the forefront of the frame. Unfortunately, the contact sheets revealed that the bottom of her shoes looked absolutely brand new—not even one mark. Since the dead body was supposed to have been a streetwalker, the pristine shoes ruined the illusion, to say the least. Instead, I went with a tight shot of her wounds.

EPISODE 275: "ATTORNEY CLIENT," ORIGINAL NBC AIRDATE: MAY 8, 2002 (PAGE 101)
This was the first crime scene to be shot in downtown Manhattan after 9/11; the Tribeca location was only a few blocks north of Ground Zero. In the night, the memorial tower lights that had recently been installed were clearly visible. For the first time, pedestrians who stumbled upon us shooting did not hang around to watch. Instead, they asked for directions to the Trade Center site. It was strange and disquieting.

EPISODE 238: "HUBRIS," ORIGINAL NBC AIRDATE: JANUARY 10, 2001 (PAGES 102 & 103)

For this crime scene, the art department created an office in a jewelry store in the Tribeca area of lower Manhattan. There were four dead bodies in the scene, which made it complicated and time-consuming. It was also very uncomfortable, particularly for the three adults who were bound and gagged with duct tape. The art director took great care in using these photographs as evidence shots on *Law & Order*, cropping out some details—especially in the photograph of the child. The shot shown here of the little girl was not used on the show, rather, one that was subtler was used. This was a difficult shoot for stills, because when I was finally given time to work, the bodies were showing signs of fatigue. The little girl, in particular, kept shifting her body. For the establishing still, I shot downward from the top of a ladder, as quickly as I could, and then moved around to each individual. I have to congratulate these actors on their dedication, because, for them, this was truly a demanding crime scene.

EPISODE 159: "DENIAL," ORIGINAL NBC AIRDATE: OCTOBER 8, 1997 (PAGE 104)

Shot in a loft in the Chelsea district of the city, this crime scene had the most blood I'd seen at any of the shoots. I can only assume that because there were no bodies on the bed, the network did not, as was the case with "Privileged," banish this episode to the shelf.

EPISODE 254: "WHO LET THE DOGS OUT?" ORIGINAL NBC AIRDATE: SEPTEMBER 26, 2001 (PAGE 105, TOP)

Filmed in Central Park, this crime scene was tempered to avoid what, according to the script, would have been too gruesome to show on air. The "victim" was mauled by a dog, so instead of showing the actual wounds, the director opted to have the audience use its imagination.

TEST SHOT (PAGE 105, BOTTOM)

Law & Order on occasion creates body parts on a per need basis for crime scenes. In this case, a rewrite for an episode suddenly required a dismembered woman's hand. Unfortunately, the prop department could only locate an old hand that had been created for a man. Thus, I did test shots to see if we could get by using a male's hand as a female's. In the end, it was used in a crime scene.

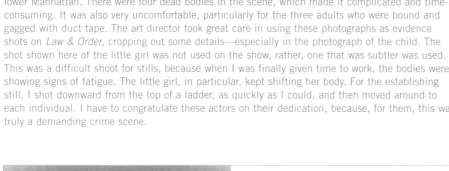

EPISODE 246: "EGO," ORIGINAL NBC AIRDATE: MARCH 21, 2001 (PAGES 106 & 107)

The "floater" was in the Hudson River at Inwood, and afforded a rare opportunity to shoot wide-angle without worry about catching any equipment or crew in the shot. Although this crime scene worked well for stills, it later had to be reshot for film. *Law & Order*, as one would suspect, uses dummies for all its floater crime scenes. This particular dummy, albeit realistic from a distance, was clearly not working in close-ups. Its "face" was plainly bizarre and despite numerous attempts at covering it with hair made from a mop, it just wouldn't cooperate. In the Aftermath, when Jerry and Jesse had to look at the "face," they had some difficulty in trying to pretend that there was nothing wrong. Ever the professionals, they worked hard not to laugh, which, though laudable, was in the end impossible.

EPISODE 172: "FACCIA A FACCIA," ORIGINAL NBC AIRDATE: FEBRUARY 25, 1998 (PAGE 108)

This was a morning shoot located at an edge of the lake in Central Park. I was struggling for a shot because there was so much crew activity going on. Ben was standing nearby and, sensing my frustration, literally gave me a hand—his gloved hand, which appears in the shot. The dead body really enjoyed himself and after the shoot pretended to be Frankenstein, growling, holding out his arms, and lunging for people's necks.

EPISODE 85: "SANCTUARY," ORIGINAL NBC AIRDATE: APRIL 13, 1994 (PAGE 109)

As I explained when first referring to this scene (page 153), this was the first *Law & Order* crime scene that I shot. Accordingly, although this photograph closes the chapter on the crime scenes, in fact, it was the first shot I ever printed for this project. To this day, Dick and I both agree that no other photograph so strongly evokes our initial excitement about documenting these graphic scenes in book form.

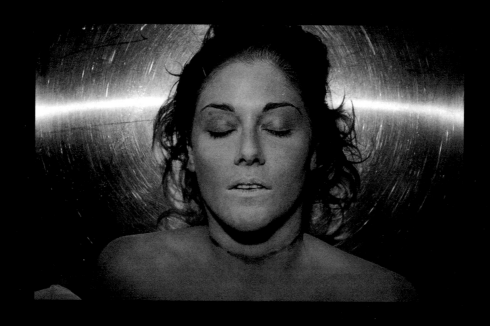

TOP: "OXYMORON" MORGUE PHOTOGRAPH, BOTTOM: A TRUE OXYMORON—A LIVE DEAD BODY

ACKNOWLEDGMENTS

Dick Wolf and Jessica Burstein gratefully acknowledge the following people: the entire crew of *Law & Order.* We wish that space allowed us to list, individually, each member of this extraordinary team. As well, the authors thank: Lydia Mayberry, Greg Wylie, Pam Golum, Audrey Davis, Joanna Giddon, Charlie Engel, Rob Harland, Neil Schubert, John Lavet, Michael Chernuchin, Woody Pirtle and his exceptional team at Pentagram Design, Charles Nurnberg, Ronni Stolzenberg, Chris Vaccari, Jason Prince, and our agent, Bill Gladstone. Most of all, we want to thank our friends at Barnes & Noble Publishing: President Alan Kahn, Publisher Michael Fragnito, Creative Director Jeffrey Batzli, Production Manager Richela Morgan, our editor, Meredith Peters, and Sharmilla Sinanan—all truly talented people, who honored their word, always.

In addition, Jessica Burstein would like to thank: Karen Burstein, for her brilliant legal services; Patricia Burnham, for her support and invaluable advice; Gene Ritchings and Nora Elcar at *Law & Order* for their generous help over the years on this project; Chad Lukaszewiski, for much of the photographic printing; Renee St. Jean, for her assistance; the entire *Law & Order* prop department, Ron Stone, Robin McCallister, Heather Kane, Julie Dubrow, and Candy Heiland; the set scenics, past and present, Eloise Meyer and Kevin Golden; also, Fred Chalfy, Harry Darrow, Marilee Mahoney, Kathy O'Connell, Sheyna Smith, Heather Brown, Carmela Spotorno, and J.R. Martin.

Law & Order Crew, 2000